ROB FEENIE'S
CASUAL CLASSICS

Everyday Recipes
for Family and Friends

ROB FEENIE'S

CASUAL CLASSICS

foreword by **Mark McEwan**

Douglas & McIntyre
D&M PUBLISHERS INC.
Vancouver/Toronto/Berkeley

Douglas & McIntyre
An imprint of D&M Publishers Inc.
2323 Quebec Street, Suite 201
Vancouver BC Canada V5T 4S7
www.douglas-mcintyre.com

Cataloguing data available from Library and Archives Canada
ISBN 978-1-55365-873-3 (pbk.)
ISBN 978-1-55365-874-0 (ebook)

Editing by Lucy Kenward
Copyediting by Pam Robertson
Cover and interior design by Peter Cocking
Front cover photos by John Sherlock
Back cover photo by Shannon Mendes
Interior photography by John Sherlock (food)
and Shannon Mendes (family)
Printed and bound in China by C&C Offset Printing Co., Ltd.
Distributed in the U.S. by Publishers Group West

We gratefully acknowledge the financial support of the Canada
Council for the Arts, the British Columbia Arts Council, the
Province of British Columbia through the Book Publishing Tax
Credit and the Government of Canada through the Canada
Book Fund for our publishing activities.

CONTENTS

PEOPLE always want to know what chefs eat at home. Some jealously imagine that we spend our nights off gorging on six-course, three-star meals. Others figure, more sensibly, that home for us is a refuge from work, like it is for anyone else, and so we probably just eat takeout and relax. The truth, of course, lies somewhere in between.

Chefs do take a break at home—but we are generally too preoccupied with what lands on the table to cede the kitchen entirely. So, we kick back and cook something a little simpler, a bit more robust and a lot less fussed over than we would at work. There's no fancy plating—just big platters to be divided and enjoyed at table, however gathered family and guests choose to do it. It's a casual approach, in other words, but one without a compromise in flavour. That's the way I do things anyway, because these festive pleasures of the family table are what got me into the business in the first place.

Reading this newest book by Rob Feenie, it is immediately clear that he feels exactly the same way. It does not surprise me, because I know this is the kind of food he has been working on at Cactus Club. And, more personally, because I have had the pleasure of cooking with him, alternating courses for a special meal at my restaurant Bymark one night, and that experience left me with a pretty good understanding of the way he does things. To my way of thinking, he does them right.

What you see in these recipes from his home are imaginative, brightly flavoured dishes that integrate lots of great culinary traditions, all explained with personal, anecdotal stories that, like the food itself, never muddle the point. And the essential point is this: you can always eat very well at home, even without investing too much time in the kitchen. Just buy the best ingredients, and have a good plan. A plan, like so many of the recipes in these pages, that makes the most of your ingredients but leaves you with plenty of time for enjoying the meal at the table with friends and family. Because good food shared with those we love is what dining should be all about— for chefs, and for all of us.

MARK MCEWAN
*Owner of North 44, Bymark, One and Fabbrica in Toronto
and Head Judge of Top Chef Canada*

Introduction

As a wise woman, my mother, once told me, the most important ingredient in food is love. Without it, food means nothing.

Love is in the work I do as a chef, cooking with my very heart and soul. For me it is a thrill to create dishes every day that might be the greatest meal someone has ever tasted. Love is in the passion of the people I work with now and have worked with over the course of my career. And love is shown in the hard work and commitment of the Canadian farmers and producers whose quality local foods and wines are helping make this country one of the best food spots in the world.

I've always loved simple food prepared with care and quality, made with fresh ingredients and served in a fun, unstuffy, welcoming environment. And I've always believed that shopping for the best-quality local products means being able to eat well without spending too much money, and being able to have fun doing it. Those beliefs are what this book is about.

This is my fourth cookbook. Each book, I hope, has drawn you a little more into my world and my food philosophies. My books are not about following trends—though I like to think I help set those trends!—but they celebrate the broad range of discoveries and influences I was experiencing at the time of writing.

When I wrote *Rob Feenie Cooks at Lumière* in 2001, I had just opened my own fine-dining room and was eager to share my love of British Columbia's seasonal ingredients prepared using French techniques and Asian flavours. Then came *Lumière Light* and *Feenie's*, both of which continued my focus on Canadian foods but with dishes that were prepared more simply and influenced by my travels in Europe and Asia and my time on *Iron Chef America*.

This book brings you to where I am today. I am now part of the Cactus Restaurant group, the leader in Western Canada's casual but fine-dining movement. Casual, sophisticated dining is not a new idea—it's been around for years—but it's certainly become a more widely recognized and celebrated concept. The increasing availability of top-quality, locally sourced food and wine is helping to ensure that casual fine dining continues to grow. To me, it's the future of North American dining.

So, this book is entirely filled with casual, sophisticated recipes that call for fresh, delicious and healthy local products, prepared simply and designed to be enjoyed in a fun, let's-get-together-type atmosphere. In fact, many of these recipes were inspired while I was barbecuing on the back deck of our summer retreat in the Okanagan, or just hanging out in the kitchen with family, close friends and even other helpful chefs who constantly suggested I add a little of this or a little of that to turn a good dish into a great experience.

Some of these recipes were also inspired by the many great chefs I have worked with over the years. Besides teaching me many special cooking techniques, they have taught me how to appreciate tradition and put flavour first in any dish I create. They have shown me that sourcing local products and supporting local producers and suppliers benefits us all. And above all, they have shown me that it is a passion for food and a love of cooking that produces truly memorable dishes.

For this knowledge, I thank Charlie Trotter in Chicago, who pushed me to a whole new level. Also Michel Jacob here in Vancouver, and Johnny Letzer and Emile Jung in Alsace, who taught me to understand, appreciate and celebrate tradition and consistency. And thank you to the late Santiago "Santi" Santamaria, one of the greatest chefs of our time, who believed I had the love it takes to make a great chef, and kindly told me as much.

Thanks are due to Richard Jaffray, founder and president of Cactus Restaurants and a long-time friend. I have always admired and looked up to Richard, and now I thank him for giving me a new life—and a new challenge—four years ago. He has built a wonderful team, and they have become an extended family to me as they continually push me and themselves to be better and better. In particular I would like to thank Christy Murphy for her unconditional support; Jim Stewart, who as a lifelong friend is also an unfailingly positive influence in my life; and Jasmin Porcic, who works closely with me to develop the recipes for Cactus Restaurants and also assisted with the ones on the pages that follow. And a personal thank you to Joan Cross, who has helped me a lot in creating this book. She is one of the most amazing women I know.

Most importantly, I want to acknowledge my thanks and my love to my beautiful wife, Michelle, and my three angels, Devon, Jordan and Brooklyn. You are, quite simply, my reasons for being.

To you, my readers, enjoy these recipes; I share them from my heart. Each recipe is a food memory to me, and memories are for sharing. I hope they help you create, stir and share memories of your own.

ROB FEENIE

APPETIZERS

Appetizer *Platter*

Boiled artichokes

2 lemons

1 tsp salt

12 to 15 small fresh artichokes

O N   A   T R I P to Spain several years ago, I gained a huge respect for tapas. The small shared dishes are perfect for dinner parties when you are looking for something everyone can enjoy. Make all of these tapas or just a few of them to serve before dinner or with drinks.

The grilled peppers are one of my specialties, and I have added some tomatillos for a small twist. Serve the olives and artichokes as part of this antipasto platter, or use them in salad, on pizza or as a side dish with roasted chicken. The oven-dried tomatoes are little gems that have followed me for quite some time because their flavour is so simple you can use them in many ways. The pickled beets most resemble an English beetroot, and they are also a nice side dish with most sandwiches or an excellent complement to cold or hot pork dishes.

Making hummus with fava beans instead of chickpeas results in a brilliant green colour and a lighter, fresher flavour. Serve this hummus on crostini or simply with fresh vegetables. The eggplant caviar can be served as a dip with some crusty bread or baked pita chips or as an excellent side dish for either roasted lamb or veal. The delightful, colourful relish is a delicious combination of sweet prawns and tangy lemons. Serve the blue cheese–stuffed figs with chicken, pork or fish or with a cheese course at the end of a meal. Each individual appetizer serves 6

Boiled artichokes Bring a large pot of water to a boil on high heat. Add the juice of 1 lemon and the salt. Using a small paring knife, trim the tough outer leaves and stems from the artichokes. Continue paring the leaves down until you reach the tender light-coloured heart. Remove the fuzzy choke, if present, with a small spoon. Cut the second lemon in half and rub all surfaces of the artichoke hearts to prevent discolouration. Place the hearts in the boiling water and cook for 2 minutes. Remove from the heat and drain in a colander. Serve warm.

To store leftover artichokes, stir in the juice of 1 lemon and 1 Tbsp extra-virgin olive oil and refrigerate in an airtight container for 4 to 5 days.

Grilled red peppers and tomatillos

2 whole red bell peppers

2 whole tomatillos, husks removed

1 tsp extra-virgin olive oil

Oven-dried tomatoes

12 Roma tomatoes

1 tsp salt

3 cloves garlic, peeled and crushed

8 sprigs fresh thyme

½ cup extra-virgin olive oil

Grilled red peppers and tomatillos Turn on the barbecue to high. Lightly rub bell peppers and tomatillos with olive oil, then place directly on the barbecue. Grill tomatillos until lightly charred but firm, 2 to 3 minutes. Using a slotted spoon, remove tomatillos from the barbecue and transfer to a clean work surface to cool slightly. Use tongs to rotate bell peppers, grilling on all sides until the skins are evenly charred, 4 to 5 minutes. Remove from the barbecue and transfer to a large bowl. Cover tightly with plastic wrap, allowing bell peppers to steam for 5 to 10 minutes. This makes it easier to peel off the skins.

Using your fingers, peel tomatillos, discarding the skins, and cut in ½-inch dice.

Remove the plastic wrap from the bowl of bell peppers and use your fingers to peel off and discard the skins. Using a sharp knife, cut bell peppers in half and remove the seeds, discarding them. Cut the flesh in ½-inch dice. Mix tomatillos and bell peppers. Will keep refrigerated in an airtight container for up to 2 days.

Oven-dried tomatoes Fill a large bowl with ice water. Bring a large pot of water to a boil on high heat. Blanch tomatoes for 10 to 20 seconds. Using a slotted spoon, remove tomatoes and immediately plunge them into the ice water. Allow them to cool.

Preheat the oven to 250°F. Line a baking sheet with parchment paper.

Remove tomatoes from the ice water. Using your hands, peel and discard the skins. With a sharp knife, slice tomatoes in half lengthwise; remove and discard the seeds. (When you seed the tomatoes, hold them over a bowl to catch all the juices. Pour the contents of the bowl through a fine-mesh sieve, discard the seeds and enjoy the resulting tomato juice.) Place tomatoes, cut side up, on the baking sheet and season with salt. Scatter garlic and thyme over the tomatoes and drizzle with olive oil. Roast tomatoes for 6 to 8 hours, until wrinkled and almost dry. Remove from oven, discard thyme and allow to cool.

Refrigerate tomatoes in an airtight glass or ceramic container, along with the oil from the baking sheet, for up to 3 days (or, drizzled with more olive oil, for up to 1 week).

Pickled beets

1 lb beets, scrubbed and green tops trimmed, unpeeled

4 cups unsweetened apple juice

1 cup rice vinegar

1 sprig fresh rosemary

1 Tbsp coriander seeds

1½ tsp mustard seeds

⅔ cup granulated sugar

1 Tbsp salt

Fava bean hummus

2 cups shelled fava beans

2 Tbsp tahini paste

2 cloves garlic, finely chopped

Juice of 1 lemon (about 2 Tbsp)

½ cup extra-virgin olive oil

Fava bean hummus Bring a medium pot of salted water to a boil on high heat. Add beans and cook for about 5 minutes, or until fork tender. Remove from the heat and drain beans in a colander.

In a food processor, combine beans, tahini paste, garlic and lemon juice. Blend on high speed. With the motor running, slowly add olive oil in a thin stream until the mixture is slightly runny like nut butter but thick enough to hold its shape. (If hummus seems too thick, add another 1 to 2 Tbsp olive oil or water.) Season with salt.

Transfer hummus to a bowl and serve, or refrigerate in an airtight container for up to 1 week.

Pickled beets Preheat the oven to 400°F. Place beets in a large roasting pan and cover with aluminum foil. Bake until tender, 30 to 60 minutes depending on the size of the beets. Check doneness by inserting a thin-bladed knife into the centre of one. Remove from the oven and allow to cool slightly.

Using paper towels, gently rub the still-warm beets all over to remove their skins. Discard the skins and set beets aside.

In a large pot, combine apple juice, rice vinegar, rosemary, coriander seeds, mustard seeds, sugar and salt and bring to a boil on medium-high heat. Reduce the heat to low and simmer for 5 minutes to develop the flavours.

While the pickling liquid is simmering, slice the peeled beets in any shape you like and place them in a glass or ceramic container with a lid. Pour the hot pickling liquid overtop and allow to cool completely.

Cover cooled beets and refrigerate in an airtight container for up to 2 weeks. These pickled beets are best served at room temperature.

Eggplant caviar

2 large globe eggplants,
1¾ to 2 lbs total weight

2 Tbsp kosher salt

2 cloves garlic, minced

¼ cup extra-virgin olive oil

½ large onion, in ¼-inch dice

2 large red bell peppers, in ¼-inch dice

½ cup dry white wine

3 Tbsp honey

¼ cup finely chopped fresh
flat-leaf parsley

Marinated black olives

1 cup large unpitted black olives
(oil-marinated Kalamatas are best)

Zest of 1 lemon, finely grated

1 tsp chopped fresh thyme

½ tsp coarsely ground black pepper

1 Tbsp extra-virgin olive oil

Eggplant caviar Place a wire cooling rack over a large baking sheet. Using a sharp knife, cut eggplants in half lengthwise and score the white flesh about ¼ inch deep in a criss-cross manner. Sprinkle salt over the scored sides of the eggplant halves, then place them cut side down on the wire rack. Allow eggplants to sit for 30 minutes. Hold eggplants under running water to rinse off salt, then gently squeeze out excess moisture and pat eggplants dry with paper towels.

Preheat the oven to 375°F and line a baking sheet with parchment paper. In a small bowl, mix garlic and 3 Tbsp of the olive oil. Brush the mixture over the scored sides of the eggplants, then place eggplants, cut side down, on the baking sheet. Roast for about 30 minutes, or until tender. Remove from the oven and allow to cool.

Using a spoon, scoop eggplant flesh onto a clean cutting board, discarding the skins. Chop eggplant flesh with a sharp knife, then transfer to a medium bowl and reserve.

In a pot on medium-low, heat the remaining olive oil. Add onions and bell peppers and cook until tender but not brown, about 15 minutes. Stir in eggplant flesh, white wine and honey. Season with salt and black pepper and continue to cook on medium heat for 15 minutes, or until thick. Remove from the heat and allow to cool.

Just before serving, stir in parsley. Serve caviar at room temperature. Refrigerate leftovers in an airtight container for up to 4 days.

Prawn and lemon relish

1 Tbsp + 2 tsp extra-virgin olive oil

6 large prawns, peeled and deveined

¼ tsp sea salt mixed with a pinch of freshly ground white pepper

¼ cup peeled, seeded and chopped fresh tomatoes

¼ cup diced preserved lemons

2 Tbsp capers, rinsed

3 tsp finely chopped fresh tarragon

3 tsp finely chopped fresh flat-leaf parsley

½ tsp sherry vinegar

½ tsp black olive tapenade

Blue cheese–stuffed figs

10 fresh Black Mission figs (about 1 lb)

4 oz soft blue cheese

⅓ cup coarsely chopped walnuts

⅓ cup honey

1 tsp lemon zest

1 tsp finely chopped fresh flat-leaf parsley

Marinated black olives Toss olives, lemon zest, thyme, black pepper and olive oil in a medium bowl and allow the flavours to infuse at room temperature for at least 10 minutes (2 days, refrigerated, is best). Refrigerate in a covered glass container for up to 1 month, but allow to stand at room temperature half an hour before serving.

Prawn and lemon relish Heat a sauté pan on medium-high and add 1 Tbsp of the olive oil. When oil is hot, add prawns, season with the salt and white pepper mixture and cook for 1 to 2 minutes, stirring, until prawns are bright pink. They should feel slightly firm. Remove from the heat and transfer prawns to a plate to cool. Pour any pan juices into a bowl.

Add tomatoes, lemons, capers, tarragon, parsley, sherry vinegar and the remaining olive oil to the bowl.

Roughly chop prawns and add to the tomato mixture. At this point, relish can be refrigerated in an airtight container for up to 3 days. Just before serving, stir in tapenade.

Blue cheese–stuffed figs Preheat the oven to 350°F. Using a sharp knife, cut an X into the top (stem end) of each fig. Cut deeply into the fruit without cutting all the way through. With your fingers, gently squeeze open each fig like a flower.

In a small bowl, mix blue cheese and walnuts until thoroughly combined. Stuff each fig with a heaping tablespoonful of the cheese mixture and arrange in an ovenproof baking dish. Drizzle with honey and bake for 10 minutes, or until figs are warm and cheese has softened. Remove from the oven and arrange on a serving platter. Just before serving, sprinkle with lemon zest and parsley. Refrigerate leftover figs in an airtight container for up to 3 days.

Steak *Tartare*

½ cup basic mayonnaise (page 158)

2 Tbsp Dijon mustard

2 Tbsp ketchup

2 Tbsp capers, rinsed
and finely chopped

1 tsp Worcestershire sauce

1 tsp Tabasco sauce

1 anchovy fillet, minced

3 Tbsp minced red onions

3 Tbsp chopped gherkins

1 clove garlic, minced

1 tsp chopped fresh chives

1 tsp chopped fresh tarragon

2 Tbsp chopped black olives

2 lbs beef tenderloin, well chilled

2 Tbsp extra-virgin olive oil

1 Tbsp good-quality cognac
(plus an ounce per person
to serve on the side, if desired)

1 sourdough baguette,
sliced and toasted

MY CLOSE family friend Randy Zien loves steak tartare, and we often eat it with a good ounce of cognac on the side! This recipe takes me back to my early twenties, when I was working in France with Johnny Letzer, now a friend and one of the greatest chefs I know. The key ingredients are the anchovy, the cognac and the ketchup. Also, be sure to use beef tenderloin here, and keep it very cold so it's easier to cut. And serve a shot glass of cognac to each guest to pour on their tartare if desired. Serves 10 to 20

Refrigerate a large bowl for 20 minutes, or until chilled. Add mayonnaise, mustard, ketchup, capers, Worcestershire sauce, Tabasco sauce, anchovies, onions, gherkins, garlic, chives, tarragon and olives to the bowl and mix until thoroughly combined. Set aside in the refrigerator.

Using a very sharp clean knife and clean cutting board, finely chop beef into an even ⅛-inch dice.

To serve, fill a large serving bowl with ice. Fold beef into the mayonnaise mixture, then stir in olive oil and the 1 Tbsp cognac and season with fine sea salt and freshly ground black pepper. Transfer the tartare to a serving bowl smaller than the bowl of ice. Set the bowl of tartare in the bowl of ice. Arrange the toasted baguette slices in a basket on the side. Encourage guests to serve themselves immediately.

Ahi Tuna *Tartare*

with a Soy and Lemon Dressing
and Sambal Mayonnaise

6 oz sashimi-grade ahi tuna, chilled

1 tsp light Japanese soy sauce

1 tsp rice vinegar

1 tsp fresh lemon juice

1 Tbsp finely sliced green onions

1 Tbsp black sesame seeds

¼ cup sambal mayonnaise (page 159)

FRESHNESS and cleanliness are essential to making this dish. Purchase the freshest fish you can find and keep all the utensils, the cutting surface and your hands clean while preparing the ingredients. Serve this appetizer in Japanese ceramic soup spoons (or won ton spoons, which are available at dollar stores). **Makes 12 spoons**

Using a very sharp knife, slice tuna in ½-inch dice. (To prevent your knife from sticking to the fish, rinse the knife in cold running water before each slice.) Place tuna in a bowl and refrigerate, covered, while you prepare the remaining ingredients.

In a medium bowl, combine soy sauce, rice vinegar, lemon juice and green onions. Pour this mixture into the bowl of tuna and combine gently until fish is well coated. Add sesame seeds and mix well.

Arrange 12 Japanese ceramic spoons on a large platter. Place 1 Tbsp of tuna in each spoon and top each serving with a dollop of spicy mayonnaise. Serve immediately (and discard rather than refrigerate leftovers).

Pizza *Three Ways*

Margherita, Rustica,
Spicy Sausage and Mascarpone

Pizza dough

1 cup lukewarm water (about 115°F)

1 Tbsp dry yeast

4 Tbsp honey

4 Tbsp extra-virgin olive oil +
2 tsp, for greasing

3¼ cups all-purpose flour

1 tsp salt

EVERYONE loves pizza. And the honey in this dough makes it so delicious you will not need another recipe. Make small pizzas as appetizers or larger ones for casual get-togethers, then top them with your favourite ingredients. Master this recipe: you will use it over and over. Makes four 10-inch pizzas

CHEF'S TIP When working with pizza dough, rub a light coating of olive oil on your hands to prevent the dough from sticking to them. This may also prevent the dough from breaking as you stretch it.

Pizza dough In a small bowl, combine water, yeast, honey and the 4 Tbsp olive oil. Allow to rest in a warm place until the yeast activates, 5 to 15 minutes. The thick foam that appears on top of the liquid is proof that the yeast is activated.

Lightly grease a large bowl with olive oil. Cut a 12-inch sheet of plastic wrap.

Add flour and salt to the bowl of a heavy-duty mixer with a dough hook. Blend on low speed until well combined, then slowly add the liquid and mix until a ball forms and the dough no longer sticks to the side of the bowl. Transfer the dough to the large bowl and cover with the plastic wrap, placing it directly on the ball of dough. Allow to rest at room temperature until doubled in size, about 10 minutes. Lightly grease a baking sheet with olive oil.

Lightly dust a clean work surface with flour. Place the ball of dough on top and remove the plastic wrap. Punch down the dough and knead by hand for 1 minute, until smooth, then divide into four 6-oz balls. Arrange dough balls on the baking sheet and loosely cover them with plastic wrap. (If you are making the dough ahead of time, lightly rub the balls with olive oil, wrap them tightly in plastic wrap and refrigerate for up to 2 days or freeze for up to 1 month. Thaw frozen dough overnight in the refrigerator before proceeding.)

Continued overleaf >

Pizza margherita

¼ recipe pizza dough (page 15)

¼ cup tomato and basil sauce (page 161)

4 oz bocconcini mozzarella,
in ¼-inch slices

4 fresh basil leaves, torn in half

2 tsp extra-virgin olive oil

1 Tbsp freshly grated Parmesan cheese

1 tsp balsamic reduction (page 159)

Maldon salt

Margherita This truly original variation on the traditional, simple tomato sauce pizza has three basic ingredients representing the three colours of Italy: red tomato sauce, white bocconcini cheese and green basil. (For a meaty version, you can also add four or five pieces of prosciutto just before you cut the pizza.) Use the best-quality ingredients you can find. Makes one 10- to 12-inch pizza

Flatten a ball of dough with the palm of your hand. Using a rolling pin, roll the dough into a 10- to 12-inch circle. Handstretch the dough slightly to create a "rustic," uneven edge. Place pizza shell on a perforated pizza tray or any thin baking sheet, stretching the dough to fit and folding the edge under to make a little rim.

Preheat the oven to 450°F. Spread pizza shell with tomato sauce, leaving ¼ inch bare all around the edge. Arrange mozzarella slices over the sauce, then top with basil. Bake for 3 minutes and remove from the oven.

Using a pastry brush, paint 1 tsp of the olive oil around the edge of the pizza. This will create a crispy crust. Return to the oven and bake for an additional 3 minutes, or until the crust is golden and the cheese is bubbling.

Remove from the oven and sprinkle with Parmesan cheese. Drizzle the remaining olive oil over the pizza, then drizzle with balsamic reduction in a zigzag pattern. Sprinkle lightly with Maldon salt.

Transfer the pizza to a cutting board and use a sharp knife to cut it into 6 slices.

Rustica This pizza is inspired by a very basic version I had on a trip to Naples in 2000, one of the first really memorable pizzas I've eaten. Serve it with a good Chianti. Makes one 10- to 12-inch pizza

Flatten a ball of dough with the palm of your hand. Using your hands, roughly fashion the dough into a 10- to 12-inch circle. Handstretch the dough slightly to create a "rustic," uneven edge. Place pizza on a perforated pizza tray or any thin baking sheet, stretching the dough to fit and folding the edge under to make a little rim.

Preheat the oven to 450°F. Spread pizza shell with tomato sauce, leaving ¼ inch bare all around the edge. Dollop spoonfuls of ricotta cheese evenly over the tomato sauce, then top with ham and mozzarella. Bake for 3 minutes and remove from the oven.

Pizza rustica

¼ recipe pizza dough (page 15)

¼ cup tomato and basil sauce (page 161)

⅓ cup ricotta cheese

1 oz shaved ham (2 to 3 slices)

3 oz mozzarella, in six 1- × 2-inch pieces

2 tsp extra-virgin olive oil

2 Tbsp roughly chopped fresh basil

Spicy sausage and mascarpone pizza

¼ recipe pizza dough (page 15)

¼ cup tomato and basil sauce (page 161)

½ cup spicy sausage and mascarpone mixture (page 19)

2 Tbsp ricotta cheese

2 tsp extra-virgin olive oil

1 tsp balsamic reduction (page 159)

1½ tsp chopped fresh flat-leaf parsley

1½ tsp chopped fresh thyme

Using a pastry brush, paint 1 tsp of the olive oil around the edges of the pizza. This will create a crispy crust. Return to the oven and bake for an additional 3 minutes, or until the crust is golden and the cheese is bubbling.

Remove from the oven and sprinkle with basil, then drizzle with the remaining olive oil. Transfer the pizza to a cutting board and use a sharp knife to cut it into 6 slices.

Spicy sausage and mascarpone I am lucky to have travelled the world and tasted some of the best pizza in Naples, New York and Los Angeles, just to name a few places. Without a wood-burning *forno* (oven) you will not be able to match these traditional pizzas, but keep it simple and you'll get great results. Makes one 10- to 12-inch pizza

Flatten a ball of dough with the palm of your hand. Using a rolling pin, roll the dough into a 10- to 12-inch circle. Place pizza on a perforated pizza tray or any thin baking sheet, stretching the dough to fit and folding the edge under to make a little rim.

Preheat the oven to 450°F. Spread pizza shell with tomato sauce, leaving ¼ inch bare all around the edge. Top with the sausage mixture and dot with small clusters of ricotta cheese. Bake for 3 minutes and remove from the oven.

Using a pastry brush, paint 1 tsp of the olive oil around the edge of the pizza. This will create a crispy crust. Return to the oven and bake for an additional 3 minutes, or until the topping is bubbling hot.

Remove from the oven and drizzle with the remaining olive oil. Then drizzle balsamic reduction in a zigzag pattern over the pizza. Combine parsley and thyme in a small bowl and sprinkle over the pizza.

Transfer pizza to a cutting board and use a sharp knife to cut it into 6 slices.

Trio of **Crostini**

Spicy Sausage and Mascarpone
Creamy Mushroom and Arugula
Savoury Tomato and Parmesan

Basic crostini

1 good-quality artisanal
baguette, in ½-inch slices

3 Tbsp extra-virgin olive oil

Pinch of salt

Spicy sausage
and mascarpone

1½ tsp extra-virgin olive oil

½ lb Italian pork
sausages (mild or hot)

1 small shallot, minced

4 oz mascarpone cheese

1 Tbsp chopped
fresh flat-leaf parsley

½ tsp salt

½ tsp chili flakes

2 Tbsp balsamic
reduction (page 159)

Creamy mushroom
and arugula

⅓ cup extra-virgin olive oil

⅓ cup diced red onions

3 cups crimini mushrooms,
cleaned and thickly sliced

⅓ cup dry white wine

1 Tbsp balsamic vinegar

1 Tbsp chopped
fresh flat-leaf parsley

¼ tsp + ⅛ tsp Maldon salt

1 cup soft goat
cheese, crumbled

1 cup arugula

Juice of ½ lemon
(about 1 Tbsp)

Savoury tomato
and parmesan

3 Tbsp extra-virgin olive oil

2 tsp balsamic vinegar

¼ cup chopped basil

¼ cup finely diced red onions

½ tsp Maldon salt

¼ tsp freshly ground
black pepper

½ oven-dried tomato
(page 7) for each crostini

⅓ cup freshly grated
Parmesan cheese

I HAVE learned to love coming up with tasty, addictive and quick starters, a part of the meal I've forgotten more often than not in the past. These crostini, or little toasts, can be a meal at lunchtime or a quick snack, but I prefer to serve them as an appetizer to an Italian-themed meal. You can also use them as croutons with soup.

The toppings are versatile and can be used on crostini (or warmed flatbread), pizza, crackers, puff pastry, etc., to make quick canapés or heartier snacks. You can also vary the type of bread. Serves 6 to 8

Basic crostini Preheat a barbecue or stovetop grill to medium-high. Arrange bread slices in a single layer and grill until lightly browned. (Or arrange bread slices in a single layer on a baking sheet, brush with olive oil and toast in a 425°F oven for 2 minutes per side, or position rack 4 inches below broiler and grill for 30 seconds on each side until golden.) Remove from the heat and brush one side of the slices with olive oil and sprinkle with salt. Top each with 1 Tbsp of your favourite topping. *Continued overleaf >*

Spicy sausage and mascarpone My good friend Chef Jasmin Porcic made this dish for me one afternoon at his house, and I immediately had to know what made it so tasty. The key is putting pork and cheese together. Forget about the calories and the fat here and just enjoy.

In a frying pan, heat olive oil on medium-high and add sausages. Break up sausages into small pieces using a wooden spoon and cook for 5 minutes. Add shallots and continue cooking for 10 minutes, or until sausage is no longer pink. Remove from the heat and use a spatula to fold in mascarpone cheese and parsley. Season with salt and chili flakes. Allow to cool slightly before topping crostini. Drizzle each crostini with ½ tsp of the balsamic reduction.

Creamy mushroom and arugula The creaminess of the mushrooms along with the richness of the goat cheese in this topping is magical. Enjoy.

Heat a frying pan on medium. When it is hot, add olive oil and onions and cook, stirring, for 3 to 4 minutes, or until onions are translucent. Add mushrooms and sauté for another 5 minutes. Pour in white wine and cook until wine has evaporated, another 2 to 3 minutes, then stir in balsamic vinegar. Stir until the liquid is reduced to a few teaspoons, 2 to 3 minutes. Remove from the heat, add parsley and season with ¼ tsp Maldon salt and black pepper. Cover to keep warm and set aside.

Spoon the mushroom mixture evenly onto the crostini and top with goat cheese.

In a small bowl, toss arugula with lemon juice and season with the remaining Maldon salt and black pepper. Top crostini with arugula.

Savoury tomato and parmesan This crostini is one of the simplest but best-tasting appetizers I make, and my kids ask for it all the time. Serve the crostini as soon as you've rubbed the tomatoes onto the toasts, or they will become soggy.

In a small bowl, combine olive oil, balsamic vinegar, basil and onions. Season with Maldon salt and black pepper and set aside.

Smash half an oven-dried tomato on each crostini, then top with an equal amount of the basil-onion mixture and sprinkle with Parmesan cheese.

Barbecued Duck **Spring Rolls**

1 lb barbecued duck meat
(about 1 whole duck)

3 oz dried vermicelli (fine rice noodles)

½ cup finely chopped green onions

½ cup finely chopped cilantro

4 cups shredded cabbage
(¼ small cabbage, core removed)

3 Tbsp soy sauce

1 lb phyllo pastry, thawed (see page 22)

¼ cup vegetable oil

THESE spring rolls are a great example of how good simple Chinese food can taste. Not a week goes by that I don't drive by one of the meat markets in Chinatown and see the barbecued ducks hanging in the window. You could use barbecued pork instead, but I think the barbecued duck meat makes these rolls that much more special. If you can't find either of these barbecued meats, used braised short ribs or pork instead.

Serve these hearty appetizers with spicy ponzu sauce (page 159).

Makes 10 spring rolls

Set duck on a clean work surface and, using your hands, pull apart duck meat. Finely julienne meat (include some of the skin) and place in a medium bowl.

Place the vermicelli in a large bowl, cover with lukewarm water and soak for 5 minutes. Drain in a colander, squeezing out excess water, and mix with meat. Stir in green onions, cilantro, cabbage and soy sauce and mix gently. Set aside.

Preheat the oven to 375°F. Line a baking sheet with parchment paper.

Have a damp towel to cover the unused phyllo sheets, a pastry brush and all your ingredients ready to go. You will want to work quickly so the phyllo pastry does not dry out. Stack five sheets of phyllo pastry, one on top of the other, on a clean work surface, with the longer edge parallel to the front edge of the counter. Using a sharp knife, cut the sheets in half crosswise. You should have ten sheets, each about 9½ × 13 inches. Cover with the damp towel.

Remove one sheet of phyllo from the stack and place on your work surface with the 9½-inch side parallel to the counter edge. Using a pastry brush, lightly brush with vegetable oil. Spoon 1 cup of the duck mixture in a line along the bottom edge of the phyllo, leaving a ½-inch border along the bottom and a 1-inch border at each end. Fold phyllo over the filling, roll phyllo once away from the edge of the counter and then tuck in the ends. Roll up the remaining phyllo. You should have a roll about 1½ inches in diameter and 7½ inches long. Brush lightly with oil and place on the baking sheet, seam side down.

Repeat with the remaining phyllo and filling, until you have 10 spring rolls. Bake spring rolls for 15 to 20 minutes, or until shiny and golden brown. Serve immediately.

Ricotta, Feta and Spinach
Phyllo Rolls

3 eggs

¾ cup club soda or
any sparkling water

2 bunches spinach

1 cup crumbled feta cheese

1½ cups ricotta cheese

2 to 3 Tbsp vegetable oil

1 lb phyllo pastry, thawed

1 cup sour cream

1½ tsp baking powder

3 Tbsp melted butter

½ tsp salt

⅛ tsp black pepper

JASMIN PORCIC, Cactus Club Cafe's test kitchen chef, is a man I cannot say enough about: he has a heart of gold and a true passion for food. He served these rolls at a dinner party he threw at his house for our corporate chef, Eric Foskett, and my wife and me, and none of us could stop eating them. Jasmin, thank you for sharing this recipe.

These rolls make a great starter for a family-style dinner and can be served hot, cold or at room temperature. If you're not familiar with phyllo pastry, or filo as it's known in Britain, look for these thin pastry leaves in the freezer section of your supermarket. Thaw phyllo in the package overnight in the refrigerator or for five hours at room temperature.

You can make an optional sauce for this dish by mixing one cup of yogurt with one cup of peeled, chopped cucumber and two or three chopped green onions. Serves 8

Spinach can hold a great amount of dirt, especially near the root ends. To clean it well, cut off and discard the stems. Place spinach leaves in a large bowl (or sink) filled with cold water. Allow to soak for 10 minutes, agitating the leaves in the water. The dirt will drop to the bottom. Lift spinach out of the water with your hands and place it in a colander. Rinse under cold running water for few minutes, then drain well and dry in a salad spinner or by twirling it in a pillowcase.

Working in batches, stack 15 to 20 spinach leaves at a time on a large clean cutting board. Using a sharp knife, roughly chop it.

Mix feta, ricotta and spinach together in a large bowl until well combined.

Preheat the oven to 425°F. Lightly oil a 9- × 13-inch baking dish. Have a damp towel to cover the unused phyllo sheets, a pastry brush and all your ingredients ready to go. You will want to work quickly so the phyllo pastry does not dry out. Place one sheet of phyllo pastry on a clean work surface, its longer edge parallel to the front edge of the counter, and brush with vegetable oil. Set a second sheet of phyllo on top of the first and brush it with oil. Repeat with 2 more sheets of pastry, brushing each one with oil. You will have a stack of 4 sheets. Repeat, making 3 more stacks of 4 sheets.

Divide the cheese-spinach mixture into 4 portions. Spread one portion of the mixture evenly across the top layer of one phyllo stack. Starting at the edge closest to you, gently fold the phyllo over the filling, rolling the pastry away from you into a long cylinder (it will be the size and shape of a baguette). Be very gentle while rolling to prevent the phyllo from breaking. Repeat with the remaining filling portions and stacks of phyllo.

Use a sharp knife to cut the phyllo rolls crosswise into slices 2 inches wide. Arrange the slices in the baking dish, one cut side down, keeping them close to each other.

To make the topping, lightly whisk eggs in a medium bowl, then add club soda (or sparkling water), sour cream, baking powder, melted butter, salt and pepper and mix well. Pour this mixture over the phyllo rolls and bake for 30 minutes. Reduce the oven temperature to 350°F and bake for an additional 15 minutes. These phyllo rolls can be served immediately or refrigerated in an airtight container for up to one day. Reheat in a 325°F oven for about 10 minutes; they can be served warm or at room temperature.

Baked **Artichokes**

with Ricotta, Fontina and Truffle Oil

12 to 15 small fresh artichokes, cooked al dente (page 6), OR 3 cups broccoli or cauliflower florets, blanched for 3 minutes

4 Tbsp unsalted butter

¾ tsp salt

¼ tsp black pepper

2 tsp sweet paprika

½ small onion, in ¼-inch dice

1 clove garlic, finely minced

1 Tbsp grainy Dijon mustard

1 large egg, lightly beaten

¾ cup ricotta cheese

¾ cup grated fontina cheese (or Cheddar)

3 Tbsp panko crumbs

1 tsp truffle oil (optional)

ONE OF my favourite vegetables has always been the artichoke. Among the best I've had were in southern California when I was a young cook; at the time, I simply steamed and served them, with either lemon butter (page 157) or mayonnaise (page 158). They were a bit messy to eat, but well worth the effort.

Here, we've made it easy to enjoy the soft texture of artichokes in an appetizer or side dish that is not all that hard to prepare. If you prefer, though, you can use blanched and well-drained broccoli or cauliflower florets in place of the artichokes. Either way, this is a great side dish to go with a roasted poultry dinner, or to serve as part of an antipasto course with nice crusty bread. Serves 4 to 6

CHEF'S TIP Choose very small artichokes, which have virtually no choke, the hairy bit that sits on top of the heart. Remove any choke you find, as its texture in the mouth is most unpleasant.

Preheat the oven to 375°F. Grease a shallow 6- to 8-cup ovenproof baking dish.

Cut artichokes in quarters. Heat a medium pot on medium-low, then add 3 Tbsp of the butter and allow to melt. Stir in artichokes (or broccoli or cauliflower florets) and combine until well coated, then season with salt, pepper and paprika. Set aside.

Melt the remaining butter in a small pot on medium-high heat. Add onions and sauté until translucent, about 3 minutes. Add garlic and cook for 2 minutes more. Remove from the heat and stir onions and garlic into the artichokes (or broccoli or cauliflower). Add mustard and mix well.

Combine egg and cheeses in a medium bowl, then pour over the artichoke mixture. Transfer to a large baking dish, sprinkle with panko crumbs and bake for 20 minutes, until crumbs and cheese topping are golden brown.

Just before serving, finish with a light sprinkle of truffle oil. Serve immediately to enjoy this dish at its best, or refrigerate, covered, for up to a day.

Crab-Stuffed **Zucchini**

2 Tbsp unsalted butter
+ 1 tsp for greasing

3 medium zucchini, each 6 inches
long, halved lengthwise

½ cup finely chopped onions

1 tsp minced garlic

½ cup grated Swiss cheese,
such as Emmental or Gruyère

⅓ cup crumbled feta cheese

1 large egg, beaten

1 Tbsp all-purpose flour

1 Tbsp chopped fresh flat-leaf parsley

2 Tbsp chopped fresh dill

1 tsp sweet paprika

¼ tsp black pepper

½ tsp salt

6 oz fresh Dungeness crabmeat,
cooked and picked over for cartilage

ZUCCHINI is one of the most abundant but underused vegetables. It's one of my favourites because of how simple it is to work with and how its flavour complements rather than overwhelms delicate seafood.

This recipe combines sweet Dungeness crab and salty feta cheese as a filling, and these stuffed zucchini are to die for. They make a great appetizer or, served with a green salad, a nice light lunch. A melon baller is ideal for scooping the pulp out of the zucchini, but a small teaspoon will also do the job.

As a variation, you could fill the zucchini with eggplant caviar (page 10) or spicy sausage and mascarpone (page 19)—or use this crab stuffing in ripe tomatoes. Remove the tops of the tomatoes by slicing them off just below the stems. Scoop out the flesh (which can be saved for use in a soup or a pasta sauce) and fill the tomatoes with the crab mixture. Replace the tops at an angle, showing some filling. Serves 6 as an appetizer or a light lunch

Preheat the oven to 375°F. Grease a gratin dish large enough to just hold the zucchini in one layer.

Using a melon baller or a teaspoon, scoop the seedy pulp from each zucchini half into a medium bowl, leaving ⅓ of an inch of flesh inside each one. Arrange the zucchini halves in the gratin dish. Roughly chop pulp using a sharp knife.

Heat a frying pan on medium, add butter and allow to melt. Add onions and garlic and cook for 3 to 5 minutes, stirring often until onions start to soften. Stir in zucchini pulp. If there is any liquid coming out of the zucchini, cook for a few minutes to evaporate it. Remove from the heat, then transfer to a medium bowl and allow to cool for a few minutes. Stir in Swiss cheese, feta, egg, flour, parsley, dill, paprika, black pepper and salt until well combined. Gently fold in crabmeat.

Divide the mixture equally among the zucchini halves and bake for 30 minutes, until the filling is set and lightly browned. Serve hot.

1 lb broccoli

¼ cup unsalted butter

¼ cup all-purpose flour

½ tsp salt

⅛ tsp black pepper

1 cup whole milk

4 large egg yolks

1 tsp fresh lemon juice

⅛ tsp nutmeg

4 large egg whites

¼ tsp cream of tartar

THIS dish is a great way to get kids to eat broccoli and it makes a nice light dinner. You can also serve these soufflés as an appetizer or a side dish with poached chicken (page 108). Soufflés have a reputation for being difficult, but this recipe is foolproof enough that I use it when I train my Red Seal chefs. This broccoli version is the best, but you could use cauliflower instead and replace the nutmeg with a dash of curry powder. Serves 4

Using a small knife, cut stems off broccoli very close to the florets. (The stems are not used in this recipe. Wrap them in plastic wrap and reserve them for soup.) Cut florets in ¼-inch pieces (about 4 cups).

Fill a large bowl with ice water. Bring a large pot of salted water to a boil on high heat, add broccoli and cook for 3 to 4 minutes, until barely tender. Remove from the heat and drain broccoli in a colander, discarding the cooking water. Place the colander in the ice water to preserve the broccoli's bright green colour and stop it from cooking further.

Heat a large pot on medium. Add butter and allow it to melt. Stir in flour, salt and black pepper until the mixture is smooth and bubbly. Cook, stirring for 2 to 3 minutes longer, then gradually whisk in the milk. Continue cooking, stirring constantly, until the sauce coats the back of a spoon, 6 to 8 minutes. Remove from the heat.

Beat egg yolks lightly in a medium bowl. Whisking briskly, gradually add half of the hot milk mixture to the beaten yolks. Return the egg mixture to the pot and blend well. Stir in lemon juice, nutmeg and broccoli. Set aside.

Preheat the oven to 400°F. Grease four 1-cup ovenproof ramekins and place them in a large baking pan. Bring a kettle full of water to a boil.

In a mixing bowl, beat egg whites with cream of tartar until soft peaks form. Gently fold egg whites into the broccoli mixture. Fill the ramekins three-quarters full, then carefully fill the baking pan with enough boiling water to reach halfway up the sides of the ramekins. Bake for 45 to 50 minutes, until the soufflés are puffed and golden brown. Serve immediately.

SOUPS & SANDWICHES

Leek, Tomato and
Garlic Soup

Caramelized garlic

2 Tbsp extra-virgin olive oil

1 cup garlic cloves, peeled

2 Tbsp honey

½ cup vegetable stock

Croutons

1 baguette, in ¼-inch slices

¼ cup extra-virgin olive oil

2 cloves garlic, sliced in half

Soup

2 Tbsp + 2 tsp extra-virgin olive oil

1 onion, finely chopped

5 leeks, white and light green parts only, washed well and finely chopped

one ½-inch piece fresh ginger, peeled and finely minced

1 tsp minced garlic

4 cups vegetable stock

3 bay leaves

1 Thai red chili, cut in half

Pinch of cayenne pepper

4 cups peeled, seeded and diced fresh tomatoes OR two 14-oz tins Roma tomatoes, puréed and passed through a fine-mesh sieve

1½ tsp salt

4 quail eggs (optional)

As a kid, my favourite soup was tomato. And when I was a young cook, I was always making soups. Here is a simple, creamy tomato soup—with optional croutons and quail eggs, if you want to take this soup to the next level. Serves 4

Caramelized garlic Heat a frying pan on medium and add olive oil. When hot, add garlic cloves and sauté, stirring, until golden brown, about 2 minutes. Add honey and toss to coat. Continue cooking garlic until it is dark brown and starting to caramelize, 4 to 5 minutes. Stir in vegetable stock and bring to a boil, then reduce the heat to low and cook until garlic is extremely soft, 15 to 20 minutes. Remove from the heat, allow to cool and refrigerate in an airtight container until ready to use, or for up to 3 days, as long as it is not stored in oil.

Croutons Preheat the oven to 350°F.

Brush bread slices on both sides with olive oil and arrange in a single layer on a baking sheet. Bake until golden brown, about 5 minutes. Turn bread over and bake for 4 to 5 minutes more. Remove from the oven and allow to cool. Lightly rub croutons on one side with cut edges of the garlic. Set croutons aside until ready to use. (Croutons will keep at room temperature in an airtight container for up to 2 days.)

Soup Heat olive oil in a large pot on medium. Reduce the heat to medium-low and sauté onions, leeks, ginger and garlic until soft, 15 to 20 minutes, stirring frequently.

Add vegetable stock, bay leaves, chilies and cayenne. Stir in tomatoes and salt, then bring to a boil on medium. Reduce the heat to low and simmer for 15 to 20 minutes. Remove and discard bay leaves and chilies, then season with salt to taste.

For a smooth soup, allow to cool slightly, then purée in batches in a food processor. Pass soup through a fine-mesh sieve and discard any solids. Set aside. (Refrigerate any leftovers in an airtight container for up to 3 days.)

To serve Line a plate with a paper towel.

Crack a quail egg into a small cup. Heat a small nonstick pan on medium and add a little olive oil. When oil is hot, carefully pour 1 quail egg into pan, sunny side up, and season with salt and pepper. Cook for 1 to 2 minutes, or to taste. Transfer egg to the plate to drain. Repeat with the remaining eggs.

In each of 4 heated bowls, place a few pieces of caramelized garlic. Pour soup over the garlic and float a crouton on the surface. Top each serving with a fried quail egg. Drizzle with a small amount of olive oil and serve immediately.

Cioppino

2 Tbsp extra-virgin olive oil

1 cup diced onions

2 tsp minced garlic

1 Tbsp chopped anchovies

½ lb live Manila clams, scrubbed clean and rinsed well in several changes of cold water

½ lb live mussels, scrubbed clean and beards removed

1 Dungeness crab, claws only, shells cracked with a mallet or nutcracker (save the body meat for another use)

1 cup dry white wine

8 cups fish stock (page 154)

3 tins (each 14 oz) canned Roma tomatoes in juice, crushed by hand or with a whisk

3 Roma tomatoes, in ½-inch dice, with seeds

⅓ cup chopped fresh basil

1 large sprig fresh oregano

½ cup chopped fresh flat-leaf parsley

2 bay leaves

2 tsp sea salt

1 tsp chili flakes

1 lb red snapper, in 1-inch dice

1 lb steelhead salmon, in 1-inch dice

1 lb B.C. spot prawns, live and heads on

THIS seafood soup is a meal in itself and it gives us a chance here on the West Coast to enjoy all that our waters have to offer. Regardless of where you're located, though, use the freshest fish that is available to you (even frozen at sea, if necessary) and be sure you have a very large pot to accommodate all the bulky ingredients in this recipe. At the heart of the cioppino is the flavourful broth; the fish is just added at the last minute and cooked quickly. Serve this hearty soup in large bowls with sourdough bread. Serves 6 to 8

CHEF'S TIP If time permits, soak the clams in cold water for a few hours before rinsing them. Otherwise, rinse them repeatedly in fresh changes of water, or set them under a continuous stream of cold water, until any water coming off them is clear.

Heat olive oil in large stockpot on medium and add onions, stirring and cooking until they are translucent, 3 to 5 minutes. Add garlic and anchovies and cook briefly, about 1 minute, then add clams, mussels and cracked crab claws. Stir well and pour in white wine, then add fish stock and canned and fresh tomatoes. Bring to a gentle simmer, then add basil, oregano, 6 Tbsp of the parsley, bay leaves, sea salt and chili flakes. Reduce the heat to medium-low and cook for about 15 minutes.

Using a slotted spoon, discard any clams and mussels that have not opened. Add snapper, salmon and prawns, increase the heat to medium-high and bring back to a boil. Reduce the heat to low and simmer for 5 to 7 minutes, until fish and prawns are cooked. Remove and discard the bay leaves and the oregano stem. Season, if necessary, with sea salt and garnish with the remaining parsley. Serve immediately. Will keep refrigerated in an airtight container for up to 1 day.

West Coast **Seafood Chowder**

1 Tbsp butter

¼ lb smoked bacon, in ½-inch pieces

½ onion, in ½-inch dice (about ¾ cup)

2 ribs celery, in ½-inch dice (about ¾ cup)

1 medium carrot, in ½-inch dice (about ½ cup)

½ tsp freshly ground black pepper

1 bouquet garni (2 sprigs fresh thyme, 1 tsp chopped fresh tarragon, 3 parsley stems and 2 bay leaves wrapped in cheesecloth)

1 cup Chardonnay or other dry white wine

2 cups fish stock (page 154) or clam nectar (or a mixture)

2 cups whole milk

2 cups whipping cream

½ lb (about 2 medium) Yukon Gold potatoes, peeled, in ½-inch dice (about 1 cup)

2 tsp salt

¼ tsp white pepper

1 lb live Manila clams, scrubbed clean and rinsed well in several changes of cold water

5 oz halibut, in 1-inch pieces

5 oz steelhead salmon, in 1-inch pieces

THIS chowder is a hearty meal and well worth the time it takes to put it together. The key here is to make sure all your fish is fresh and to eat it all the same day. Serve this dish family-style in a warmed tureen, along with some good sourdough bread and a fine Chardonnay. Serves 6

CHEF'S TIP If time permits, soak the clams in cold water for a few hours before rinsing them. Otherwise, rinse them repeatedly in fresh changes of water, or set them under a continuous stream of cold water, until any water coming off them is clear.

Heat a large pot on medium heat. Add butter and bacon, and cook, stirring frequently, until crispy, 8 to 10 minutes. Add onions, celery and carrots and cook for 2 to 3 minutes until fragrant. Stir in black pepper and add bouquet garni.

Pour in white wine and stir with a wooden spoon to deglaze the browned bits on the bottom of the pan. Add fish stock (or clam nectar), milk and whipping cream, then stir in potatoes, salt and white pepper. Without increasing the heat, bring the mixture to a boil, then reduce the heat to a simmer and cover with a lid for 5 minutes. Add clams and cook for another 8 to 10 minutes, until potatoes are tender and clams have opened. (Using a slotted spoon, discard any clams that do not open.)

Just before serving, add halibut and salmon and cook for another 2 to 3 minutes (the pieces are very small and cook quickly). Remove from the heat and transfer to a tureen. Serve immediately. Will keep refrigerated in an airtight container for up to 1 day.

Easy Cream of **Chicken Soup**

with Aged White Cheddar and Garlic Croutons

Garlic croutons

½ baguette, in ¾-inch cubes

1 Tbsp extra-virgin olive oil

1 tsp chopped garlic

⅓ cup freshly grated Parmesan cheese

½ tsp cracked black pepper

Pinch of Maldon salt

Chicken soup

2 Tbsp butter, softened

2 Tbsp all-purpose flour

8 cups chicken stock (page 155)

1 cup whipping cream or whole milk

1½ cups shredded poached chicken (page 108)

½ cup grated aged white Cheddar cheese

THIS soup makes me think of my early cooking days, around age eighteen, when I was apprenticing and had to make this dish for an exam. It also reminds me of a soup my mom made with turkey around Christmastime. This easy soup has now become a staple in my own family; we make it from the basic poached chicken recipe (page 108) on cool, rainy days when we need some soul-comforting food. Serve this soup in warmed bowls. Serves 6

Garlic croutons Preheat the oven to 325°F. Place bread cubes in a medium bowl.

In a small pot, heat olive oil on medium-low, add garlic and stir constantly, to avoid burning, for 1 to 2 minutes. Pour garlic oil over the bread, toss lightly and mix in Parmesan cheese. Add black pepper and salt. Arrange bread cubes on a baking sheet and bake for 10 minutes, or until golden brown. Remove from the oven and set aside.

Chicken soup In a small bowl, combine butter and flour to form a smooth paste. Set aside.

In a large pot, bring chicken stock to a boil on medium-high heat. Reduce the heat to a simmer and stir in whipping cream (or milk). Whisk in the butter-flour mixture, then cook, stirring often, for at least 10 minutes, until flour is cooked and soup has thickened slightly. Add chicken and heat through. Season with salt to taste.

Ladle soup into bowls, top with croutons and sprinkle with Cheddar cheese. Serve immediately. Refrigerate leftover soup in an airtight container for up to 3 days or freeze it for up to 1 month.

Spot Prawn and Avocado
BLT Sandwich

Garlic and herb aioli

3 heads of garlic, unpeeled but separated into cloves, tips cut off

1 Tbsp balsamic vinegar

1 Tbsp extra-virgin olive oil

1 Tbsp finely chopped fresh parsley

1 Tbsp finely chopped fresh thyme

⅛ tsp coarse sea salt

½ cup basic mayonnaise (page 158)

3 Tbsp fresh lemon juice

Spot prawn and avocado BLT

3 large spot prawns (about 3 oz)

1 tsp extra-virgin olive oil

1 tsp chopped fresh thyme

1 thin slice prosciutto

2 slices good-quality artisanal bread (sourdough is a good choice)

3 Tbsp garlic and herb aioli

⅛ tsp salt

½ tsp finely diced jalapeño peppers

1 Tbsp chopped red bell peppers, in ¼-inch dice

2 whole leaves butter lettuce

4 slices fresh tomato

½ avocado, peeled and sliced

INSPIRED by British Columbia's local spot prawns, this is a quick and delicious variation on the traditional bacon, lettuce and tomato sandwich. The combination of sweet prawns, salty prosciutto and spicy jalapeño makes it an irresistible treat. Use fresh prawns when they are available in May, or prawns flash frozen at sea in other seasons. Even if you don't like crispy bacon, baking the prosciutto for even a short time intensifies its flavour. Use any leftover aioli on fish, chicken or pork or as a vegetable dip. Serves 1

Garlic and herb aioli Preheat the oven to 350°F.

In a small ovenproof dish or on a piece of aluminum foil, drizzle garlic with balsamic vinegar and olive oil and cover with a lid or foil (or just wrap tightly in the foil). Roast for 45 minutes or until garlic is very soft and golden brown. Remove from the oven, uncover (or unwrap) and allow to cool.

Peel garlic and place cloves on a shallow plate. Sprinkle with parsley, thyme and the ⅛ tsp coarse sea salt (this will help with the mashing).

Using a fork, mash together garlic and herbs until they form a paste. This is a rustic aioli so do not be concerned about small bits of unmashed garlic. Transfer the mixture to a small bowl, add mayonnaise and lemon juice and stir to blend. Season with sea salt and freshly ground black pepper. Will keep refrigerated in an airtight container for up to 3 days.

Spot prawn and avocado BLT Preheat the oven to 375°F.

In a small bowl, lightly coat prawns with olive oil, thyme and a little salt and pepper. Transfer to a small ovenproof pan and bake for 5 minutes, or until shells are bright pink and the flesh resists just a little when pressed. Remove prawns from the oven, then peel and refrigerate until needed.

Add prosciutto to the ovenproof pan and bake for 5 minutes. Remove from the oven and allow to cool. Crumble and set aside at room temperature.

Toast bread in a toaster until golden. Spread 1 Tbsp of the aioli on each slice of bread.

In a small bowl, mix the remaining aioli with prawns and season with the ⅛ tsp salt. Add jalapeño and red peppers and mix well to combine.

On one slice of bread, layer lettuce, tomato and the prawn mixture. Top with prosciutto and avocado. Cover with the second slice of bread. Cut the sandwich in half and serve immediately.

Best Grilled
Ham and Cheese Sandwich

1 Tbsp + 1 tsp unsalted butter

2 slices light or dark rye
or sourdough bread

1 egg

3 oz shaved ham

3 oven-dried tomatoes (page 7)

1 oz Brie cheese

1 oz Swiss cheese, such as
Emmental or Gruyère, sliced

THIS comforting dish is perfect for cold winter days. My wife is the master of this sandwich, which my daughter Jordan could eat pretty much every day. For best results, use good-quality meats and cheeses, such as prosciutto cotto and Brie, and have all your ingredients ready to go before you begin. Assemble the rest of the sandwich while you cook the egg. **Serves 1**

Preheat the oven to 350°F.

Spread ½ Tbsp of the butter on one side of each slice of bread. Heat a small nonstick frying pan on medium, then place bread, buttered sides down, in pan and toast for 1 minute until golden brown. Place one slice of the bread, buttered side down, on a baking sheet. Set the other slice of bread aside.

Add the 1 tsp of the butter to the frying pan and reduce the heat to low. Crack egg into the frying pan. Season with salt and pepper. Cook, sunny side up, for 2 minutes, or to taste.

To the bread on the baking sheet, add ham, followed by tomatoes and cheeses, then bake in the oven until cheese is melted, 3 or 4 minutes.

Slide egg, sunny side up, onto the sandwich and top with the remaining slice of bread, buttered side up. Serve immediately.

Pulled Pork **Sliders**

with Napa Cabbage and Carrot Slaw

Napa cabbage and carrot slaw

2 Tbsp white sesame seeds

2 cups shredded Napa cabbage

1 cup shredded carrots (about 1 large)

½ cup thinly sliced green onions

¼ cup coarsely chopped cilantro

2 Tbsp fresh lemon juice

1 tsp white wine vinegar

1 tsp granulated sugar

½ tsp Tabasco sauce

¼ tsp salt

⅓ cup vegetable oil

Pulled pork sliders

12 mini Portuguese buns
or any other small soft buns

12 oz dry-rubbed pork shoulder roast
(page 133), pulled (about 3 cups)

½ cup quick barbecue sauce (page 160)

½ cup barbecue mayonnaise (page 158)

2 cups Napa cabbage and carrot slaw

FOR these particular sandwiches, soft buns are key. However, while sliders are a great way to serve pulled pork, you can also make a gluten-free version using lettuce or cabbage leaves, as in Cactus Club Cafe's popular barbecued pork lettuce wraps. Or assemble a Mexican version using soft tortillas, as in the popular carnitas that are widely available at street-food stalls. **Serves 4**

Napa cabbage and carrot slaw In a small pan on medium heat, toast sesame seeds, shaking the pan frequently, for about 5 minutes. Set aside.

In a large bowl, combine cabbage, carrots, green onions and cilantro. In a small bowl, whisk together lemon juice, white wine vinegar, sugar, Tabasco sauce, salt and vegetable oil.

Just before serving, pour the vinaigrette over the cabbage mixture and toss lightly. Sprinkle with sesame seeds.

Pulled pork sliders Preheat the oven to 375°F. Arrange mini buns on a baking sheet and place them in the oven for just 2 minutes to warm them up. Remove from the oven, wrap loosely in a kitchen towel and set aside.

Combine pulled pork with ¼ cup of the barbecue sauce in an ovenproof dish and cover with aluminum foil. Warm in the oven for 3 to 4 minutes, then remove from the oven and stir well to incorporate sauce, juices and meat.

On a clean work surface, spread the bottom half of each bun with 1 tsp of the barbecue mayonnaise, top it with 2 Tbsp of the pulled pork and drizzle with 1 tsp of the barbecue sauce. Arrange 2 Tbsp of slaw on top of the meat. Spread 1 tsp of the barbecue mayonnaise on the top half of each bun, close the sliders and serve.

Asian **Sloppy Joes**

with Cabbage-Cilantro Slaw

Cabbage-cilantro slaw

2 cups shredded green cabbage

¼ cup chopped fresh cilantro

2 Tbsp rice vinegar

1 Tbsp low-sodium soy sauce

Juice of 1 lime (about 1 Tbsp)

2 Tbsp grapeseed oil

Sloppy joes

2 Tbsp grapeseed oil

2 red onions, in ¼ inch dice (about 2 cups)

1 Tbsp minced garlic

1 Tbsp minced fresh ginger

2 ribs celery, in ¼-inch dice (about ¾ cup)

1 Tbsp sambal oelek or
any hot sauce of your choice

1 lb extra-lean ground beef

1 lb ground pork

1 cup hoisin sauce

1 cup chopped fresh or
canned Roma tomatoes

Juice of 1 lime (about 1 Tbsp)

2 tsp sea salt

½ tsp black pepper

6 Portuguese buns or
any other bun of your choice

WHEN I think of sloppy joes, those ground beef sandwiches I remember eating as a kid, it reminds me of my mom preparing Hamburger Helper (yes, that's right, I have had it a few times). The key to her version was a soft bun and a drippy grey meat mix—nothing more.

This updated recipe is an Asian version made using both pork and beef. The key is to buy soft buns and warm them—in the oven if it's already on, or in the microwave for 10 seconds—to soften them up. If you don't want to make sloppy joes, use this recipe with pasta for an Asian-style spaghetti or serve it with mashed potatoes as a main course. Remember to pour off all the fat from the meat before adding the liquids. Serves 6 to 8

Cabbage-cilantro slaw Combine cabbage and cilantro in a large bowl. In a small bowl, whisk together rice vinegar, soy sauce, lime juice and grapeseed oil. Just before serving, pour the vinaigrette over the cabbage mixture and toss lightly. Will keep refrigerated in an airtight container for 2 days.

Sloppy joes Heat a large, heavy frying pan on medium-high. Add grapeseed oil and swirl the pan to spread the oil. Add onions, garlic, ginger, celery and sambal oelek and sauté, stirring often, until onions are translucent, about 5 minutes. Add ground beef and ground pork and use a wooden spoon to break meat into small pieces. Cook, stirring frequently, until meat is no longer pink, 6 to 8 minutes. Pour off and discard any fat from the meat. Add hoisin sauce,

tomatoes and lime juice, then season with salt and pepper. Reduce the heat to
medium-low and simmer for 20 to 25 minutes, stirring occasionally.

Preheat the oven to 375°F. Cut the buns in half, place them on a baking sheet
and warm for 2 minutes, or until very lightly toasted.

Arrange the bottom halves of the buns on individual plates. Spoon about
⅔ cup of the sloppy joe mixture on top of each bun, then cover with 2 to 3 Tbsp
of cabbage-cilantro slaw. Finish with the top halves of the buns. Serve immediately. Refrigerate leftover meat and slaw, separately, in airtight containers for
up to 2 days.

SALADS & SIDES

Heirloom Tomato and
Burrata Salad

7 oz burrata

6 heirloom tomatoes, of various colours, in ½-inch slices

1 large red onion, very thinly sliced in rings

16 fresh basil leaves

2 Tbsp aged balsamic vinegar

⅓ cup good-quality extra-virgin olive oil

THIS is one of the simplest salads in the book and at the same time one of the best. Make sure you buy the best tomatoes you can, very good olive oil and, of course, some fantastic burrata. On the West Coast, heirloom tomatoes appear at farmers' markets in mid to late August. If you can't find burrata, use a good-quality buffalo mozzarella. **Serves 4**

Neatly scoop about ¼ cup of burrata onto one side of each plate. Arrange tomatoes around the burrata, varying the colours, then add a layer of onion rings and a layer of basil leaves, dividing them equally among the plates. Drizzle each salad with ½ Tbsp of the balsamic vinegar and 2 to 3 tsp (or more, if desired) of the olive oil. Season with fine sea salt and freshly ground black pepper. Serve immediately.

Creamy **Coleslaw**

½ cup basic mayonnaise (page 158)

2 tsp grainy mustard

3 Tbsp sour cream

2 tsp granulated sugar

1 tsp salt

1 Tbsp red wine vinegar

2 Tbsp fresh lemon juice

1 lb green cabbage

½ cup fresh flat-leaf parsley, whole leaves (stems removed)

I HAVE always loved this simple coleslaw that my mother made when I was a kid, and it is a staple dish in my own family now. It's easy to prepare, tasty and very good for you (the parsley and cabbage are full of healthy vitamins). The key to this salad is not to cut the cabbage too thick, and to add more sugar if the dressing becomes too tart.

Coleslaw is meant to be simple, but you can give it visual appeal by mixing green and red cabbage or throwing in other crunchy vegetables such as shredded or sliced carrots, diced sweet bell peppers or sliced, unpeeled apples or radishes. Serves 6

In a small bowl, combine mayonnaise with grainy mustard and sour cream. Season with sugar and salt. Whisking constantly, slowly add red wine vinegar and lemon juice. Set aside. (Refrigerated in an airtight container, this dressing will keep for up to 1 week.)

Using a mandoline or a sharp knife, shred cabbage as finely as possible. Place cabbage in a salad bowl, add parsley and toss gently. Add dressing, mixing lightly until all of the cabbage mixture is coated. Refrigerate for 30 minutes, until chilled, or for up to 2 days.

Roasted **Cauliflower Salad**

with Sweet and Sour Vinaigrette

Sweet and sour vinaigrette

2 Tbsp white wine vinegar

1 Tbsp fresh lemon juice

1 Tbsp Dijon mustard

1 Tbsp honey or maple syrup

1 small clove garlic, minced

½ tsp salt

6 Tbsp extra-virgin olive oil

Roasted cauliflower salad

2 large bell peppers
(red, yellow or orange)

1 Tbsp + 1 tsp extra-virgin olive oil

1 large cauliflower,
in florets (about 6 cups)

1 tsp finely chopped fresh thyme

½ tsp salt

2 Tbsp chopped
fresh chives (optional)

MY KIDS and I love cauliflower. We often eat it roasted and then finished with a drizzle of olive oil, a squirt of lemon and a handful of cheese. This salad uses the same roasted cauliflower but gives it some sweet and sour elements by adding honey and lemon juice. Serve this salad chilled for two to three hours as a main course or at room temperature as a side dish with poultry.

Sweet and sour vinaigrette In a small bowl, whisk together white wine vinegar, lemon juice, mustard, honey (or maple syrup), garlic, salt and olive oil. Refrigerate in an airtight container for up to 1 week.

Roasted cauliflower salad Preheat the oven to 450°F. Lightly brush bell peppers with 1 tsp of olive oil and place on a baking sheet. Roast, turning frequently with tongs, until the skin is blistered and dark brown, about 10 minutes. Remove from the heat. Reduce the oven temperature to 400°F.

Using the tongs, transfer peppers to a bowl and cover with plastic wrap. Allow peppers to cool. Peel off and discard pepper skins and stems, then cut open peppers and scoop out and discard the seeds. Cut peppers in ½-inch strips and set aside.

In a large bowl, toss cauliflower with the 1 Tbsp of olive oil, thyme and salt. Arrange florets in a single layer on a large baking sheet and roast for 15 minutes. Shake the pan to prevent cauliflower from sticking, then roast for 10 to 15 minutes more, or until florets are lightly browned and just tender. Remove from the oven and transfer to a large bowl.

Add peppers to the cauliflower and toss gently to combine. Pour in dressing and toss again gently to coat the vegetables evenly. Sprinkle with fresh chives. Cover with plastic wrap and refrigerate for 2 to 3 hours to allow the flavours to meld. Leftover salad will keep refrigerated for up to a day.

Spinach, Bacon and
Blue Cheese Salad

Caesar dressing

1 Tbsp finely chopped anchovies

2 Tbsp minced garlic

⅓ cup fresh lemon juice

1 cup plain yogurt

1 Tbsp Dijon mustard

1 Tbsp grainy Dijon mustard

2 Tbsp capers, rinsed and finely chopped

1 Tbsp finely chopped fresh chives

½ cup finely grated Parmesan cheese

1 tsp Tabasco sauce

1 tsp Worcestershire sauce

½ tsp freshly ground black pepper

2 cups basic mayonnaise (page 158)

Spinach, bacon and blue cheese salad

1 baguette, in 2-inch dice

¼ cup extra-virgin olive oil

½ cup freshly grated Parmesan cheese

1 garlic clove, minced

2 lbs fresh spinach, washed, trimmed of large stems and dried

1 cup Caesar dressing

10 slices double-smoked bacon, cooked until crisp and crumbled

1 cup good-quality blue cheese, crumbled

1 tsp fresh lemon juice

I JUST love a good Caesar salad and make one almost every other day at home. In this variation, I use spinach with my Caesar dressing and lots of blue cheese and, of course, bacon. I like Gorgonzola, but Roquefort or Stilton would work well too.

Everyone has a favourite Caesar salad dressing, and I think this one is pretty good. I developed the original version during my Feenie's days, when we sold a ton of these salads, and I now use a variation in the signature chargrilled chicken Caesar at Cactus Club Cafe. The key to this salad is a lot of blue cheese, and lemon to finish.

This is a very rich salad but a good one, so serve it as a starter rather than a main course, to keep the portion smaller. Add chopped pears or pecans for pure decadence. Serves 4 to 6

Caesar dressing In a large bowl, mix all ingredients until well combined. Transfer to an airtight container and refrigerate for 2 days if using homemade mayonnaise or for 5 days if using a commercial mayonnaise.

Salad Preheat the oven to 375°F. In a large bowl, toss bread with olive oil, Parmesan cheese and garlic. Season with salt and freshly ground black pepper. Arrange bread cubes on a baking sheet in a single layer and bake until lightly toasted, about 5 minutes. Remove from the heat, drain on paper towels and set aside.

In another large bowl, toss spinach with the dressing. Add croutons, bacon and blue cheese. Sprinkle with lemon juice and season with salt and black pepper. Divide among 4 to 6 plates and serve immediately.

Dungeness Crab and
Green Apple Salad

¼ cup extra-virgin olive oil +
a drizzle for garnish

10 oz fresh Dungeness crabmeat, cooked,
chilled and picked over for cartilage

2 small oranges

1 large or 2 small Granny Smith apples

1 Tbsp rice vinegar

1 Tbsp fresh lime juice

1 tsp salt

¼ tsp black pepper

6 oz buffalo mozzarella, in ¼-inch slices

½ tsp Maldon salt

ONE OF my closest friends when I was growing up had a place in Birch Bay, Washington, just on the other side of the border from Vancouver. In the summer months we used to go crab fishing there almost every other day, and eat our catch with cream cheese on toasted white bread. It was oh so good. Here is a salad that tastes fresh, as if the Dungeness crab has just come out of the ocean. And the crabmeat combines perfectly with green apple. Serve as a starter salad or as a light lunch. Serves 6 to 8 as a starter or 4 as a main dish

Using a small sharp knife, cut both ends off oranges. Set an orange down on one flat end on a cutting board. Cut away the orange peel, removing all the white pith as you pare. Repeat with the second orange, and discard the peel and pith. Holding it over a bowl to catch the juices, carefully cut between the membranes of one orange, releasing each segment into the bowl. Keep each segment as intact as possible for a more attractive presentation. Discard the membranes. Repeat with the second orange and set orange segments and collected juice aside.

Peel and core apples, discarding the peel and seeds, and cut in ¼-inch dice. Pour the collected orange juice over apples to prevent them from oxidizing. Set aside.

In a medium bowl, whisk together rice vinegar and lime juice. Slowly add olive oil, whisking to emulsify the dressing.

In a large bowl, gently combine oranges, apples and crabmeat. Add vinaigrette, toss lightly and season with salt and pepper.

Divide the salad equally among serving bowls or plates. Top with buffalo mozzarella and drizzle with a little olive oil. Sprinkle Maldon salt on top of the cheese and serve immediately.

Chop-Chop **Salad**

Sherry vinaigrette

⅓ cup sherry vinegar

2 Tbsp Dijon mustard

1 Tbsp honey

2 tsp finely chopped fresh thyme

½ tsp sea salt

1 cup extra-virgin olive oil

Chop-chop salad

4 slices double-smoked
bacon, in ¼-inch dice

2 Tbsp sherry vinaigrette

Juice of ½ small lemon (about 1 Tbsp)

8 oz poached chicken
(page 108), shredded

4 small ribs celery, in ½-inch dice

1 cucumber, peeled, quartered
lengthwise, seeded and cut in
½-inch pieces (about 48 slices)

8 radishes, in ⅛-inch slices

¼ cup currants, rinsed and patted dry

1 Gala or Granny Smith apple,
in ½-inch dice

4 handfuls arugula

½ head iceberg lettuce, in 2-inch pieces

20 grape tomatoes, cut in half

½ cup crumbled blue cheese

¼ cup pecans

AT THE Tap House, one of our Cactus Club Cafe locations, we came up with
this very simple salad that is tasty, good for you and filling. Being a salad
lover, I am sometimes looking for different approaches to the salad course. Here,
we combine bite-size pieces (hence the term "chop-chop") of lots of wonderful
salad fixings. Use a good-quality Gorgonzola or Stilton. For a twist, you can
replace the chicken with shrimp, prawns or even smoked salmon. Serves 4

Sherry vinaigrette In a small bowl, combine sherry vinegar, mustard, honey,
thyme, sea salt and mix well. Add freshly ground black pepper to taste. Using
a whisk, slowly beat olive oil into the mixture until emulsified. Will keep
refrigerated in an airtight container for up to 7 days.

Chop-chop salad Line a plate with a paper towel. In a small frying pan on
medium heat, cook bacon until crisp, about 5 minutes. Use a slotted spoon to
transfer bacon to the plate to drain.

Combine the 2 Tbsp sherry vinaigrette and lemon juice in a glass jar and
shake well.

In a large salad bowl, toss together chicken, celery, cucumber, radishes,
currants, apple, arugula, lettuce, tomatoes and bacon. Add about 2 Tbsp of
the vinaigrette and lemon juice mixture. Toss until salad is moistened evenly.
Divide salad among 4 plates. Top with blue cheese and pecans.

Quinoa, Green Bean and
Tomato Salad

1 cup quinoa, washed well and drained

1½ cups water

¾ lb fresh green beans, in 1-inch pieces

½ lb very ripe Roma tomatoes (3 to 4)

1 bell pepper (any colour), in 1-inch dice

2 Tbsp capers, rinsed

4 green onions, in ½-inch slices

½ cup roughly chopped fresh basil

¾ tsp salt

2 Tbsp extra-virgin olive oil

2 Tbsp fresh lemon juice

3 Tbsp toasted pecans

ONE OF my favourite grains right now is quinoa. It is one of the most complete proteins on the planet and can work well on its own, in a salad or with other proteins. The key is to give it flavour, which we have done here with the lemon juice, capers, bell peppers and tomatoes. Thoroughly washing the quinoa before cooking it eliminates any bitterness. Use white or red quinoa or a mix of both.

Vary this salad by using a grilled pepper (page 7) in place of the fresh bell pepper, and when fresh tomatoes are not in season, try oven-dried tomatoes (page 7) instead. Use the same quantity of roasted or raw vegetables. Serve this salad at room temperature for a vegan lunch or heat it up and serve it as a side dish with poultry, quail or barbecued salmon. **Serves 4 to 6**

Combine quinoa and the 1½ cups water in a medium pot and bring to a simmer on medium heat. Reduce the heat to low, cover and cook until all the liquid is absorbed, 15 to 20 minutes. Set aside.

Fill a large bowl with ice water. Bring a large pot of salted water to a boil on high heat, add green beans and cook for 4 to 5 minutes, until barely tender. Remove from the heat and drain green beans in a colander. Place the colander in the ice water to preserve the beans' bright green colour and stop them from cooking further.

Using a sharp knife, cut tomatoes in half and gently squeeze out and discard the seeds. (It is not necessary to remove the skins for this recipe.) Cut tomatoes in ½-inch dice.

In a large bowl, combine quinoa, green beans, tomatoes, bell peppers, capers, green onions and basil. Season with salt, olive oil and lemon juice, and sprinkle with pecans. Will keep refrigerated in an airtight container for up to 2 days.

Marinated **Calamari Salad**

1 lb calamari tubes, cleaned

¼ cup extra-virgin olive oil

2 Tbsp capers, rinsed

½ small red onion, finely minced

¼ cup Kalamata olives, pitted

1 bunch cilantro, finely chopped

4 cloves garlic, finely chopped

Juice of 1 lemon (about 2 Tbsp)

2 Tbsp balsamic vinegar

1 tsp salt

¼ tsp black pepper

1 tsp chili flakes

2 grilled red, yellow or orange bell peppers (page 7), seeded, in ½-inch strips

THIS is a super-quick recipe that can be made ahead for a fast lunch or dinner. It's addictively sweet, salty, hot and sour all at the same time, and it can be dressed up on a bed of butter lettuce or used to top crostini (page 19).

Squid is very perishable and therefore available frozen rather than fresh in food stores most of the year. You can find packages of both tubes (cleaned bodies) and tentacles or just individual parts, such as rings only. Serves 4 to 6

Using a sharp knife, cut calamari tubes in ½-inch rings and rinse under cold running water to remove any excess squid ink. Set aside.

In a large bowl, combine olive oil, capers, onions, olives, cilantro, garlic, lemon juice, balsamic vinegar, salt, black pepper and chili flakes. Set aside.

Bring a large pot of salted water to a rapid boil on high heat. Add calamari and cook for 2 minutes only. Remove from the heat and drain immediately in a colander.

Stir warm calamari into the olive oil mixture. Add grilled peppers and allow to cool, stirring occasionally. Serve at room temperature. Refrigerate leftovers in an airtight container for up to 3 days.

Grilled **Corn**

with Chili and Lime Butter

1 tsp cayenne pepper

1 Tbsp finely chopped cilantro

1 cup unsalted butter, room temperature

1 Thai red chili,
seeded and finely chopped

2 shallots, finely chopped

Juice of 1 lime (about 1 Tbsp)

6 ears fresh corn, husks on

I LOVE corn when it's in season and my kids love spice, so this simple dish makes us all happy. Serve this corn as a snack, or cut the kernels off the cob and serve as a side dish with barbecued salmon, mixing in a little chili and lime butter. The compound butter will also work well with other grilled fresh vegetables, such as asparagus, green beans and carrots. Make up a batch, keep it in the refrigerator ready for a quick meal, or experiment with other compound butters (pages 156–57). If you make the butter ahead of time, remove it from the refrigerator half an hour before you plan to serve it, slice it into rounds and allow it to soften a little. Serves 6

In a small bowl, use a fork to mix butter, shallots, lime juice, cayenne, cilantro and chili. Season with salt and pepper. Transfer butter to a small serving dish.

Preheat the barbecue to high. Place corn on the barbecue and grill for 6 minutes. Turn corn over, close the lid and barbecue for another 6 minutes. Serve immediately with the flavoured butter.

Parsnip *Purée*

1 lb parsnips, peeled, in 1-inch dice

1½ cups chicken stock (page 155)

¼ cup whipping cream

2 Tbsp butter

½ tsp salt

I LOVE the silky texture of purées, and the sweetness of the parsnips makes this version one of my favourites. This versatile purée goes with many different proteins—such as fish, beef, poultry and lamb—and can be made up to a day in advance. You can also purée cauliflower, celery root, carrots, rutabaga and winter squash.

Cooking parsnips in water can lead to "waterlogging," which causes the vegetables to lose flavour and become runny when puréed. Using stock instead prevents this problem. You could also substitute vegetable stock to make a vegetarian version. Serves 4 to 6

In a large pot, combine parsnips and chicken stock. Bring to a boil on medium-high heat. Reduce the heat to medium and simmer until tender, 15 to 20 minutes. Drain, reserving the stock for another use, and pass parsnips through a potato ricer or food mill or purée in a blender on high until smooth (about 2 minutes). For an extra-silky texture, strain purée through a fine-mesh sieve.

Add whipping cream, butter and salt and mix well. Serve immediately or allow to cool, transfer to an airtight container and refrigerate until needed, or for up to 3 days.

To reheat, place in a pot on low heat and stir frequently until hot, 5 to 6 minutes.

Broccoli with Pecorino Cheese
and Lemon Juice

4 heads broccoli, in florets (about 5 cups)

2 Tbsp extra-virgin olive oil

1 cup grated Pecorino Romano cheese

1 cup grated Gruyère cheese

Juice of 1 lemon (about 2 Tbsp)

THIS is a dish I make more than three times a week because it's so easy and it's so good that my kids, between them, will eat almost two heads of broccoli at each meal! Broccoli is available all year long, cooks quickly and is very good for you. And this dish goes with almost anything, so make it a staple in your diet and your kitchen every week. Try this recipe with cauliflower, broccolini, Brussels sprouts and asparagus, too. **Serves 6**

Fill a large bowl with ice water. Bring a large pot of salted water to a boil on high heat. Blanch broccoli for 1 minute. Immediately drain broccoli in a colander and plunge into the ice water. Drain broccoli again and set aside.

Preheat the broiler. Position an oven rack about 6 inches below the element.

In a large frying pan, heat olive oil on low. Add broccoli and toss to coat well, then add the cheeses and toss lightly until warmed through, 3 to 4 minutes. Transfer the broccoli mixture to an ovenproof casserole dish and place under the broiler. Watch closely while it forms a light brown crust, 4 to 5 minutes, then remove from the oven. Squeeze lemon juice over the broccoli and serve immediately.

Creamed **Spinach**

¼ cup unsalted butter

½ cup minced shallots

1 Tbsp minced garlic

2 bunches spinach,
washed and stems removed

1 bunch watercress,
washed and stems removed

1 tsp salt

¼ tsp black pepper

1 cup whipping cream

¼ cup fresh water chestnuts,
peeled and finely chopped

THIS is a rich comfort food that is so darn good you have to try it even if you think you don't like spinach. Serve this spinach as a side dish with grilled meats, especially steak or pork tenderloin. You can make it in advance, refrigerate it an airtight container for up to two days or freeze it for one month, so it's ready when you need it. Look for fresh water chestnuts in Asian markets. Serves 4 to 6

In a large frying pan, melt butter on medium heat. Add shallots and garlic and cook for 2 to 3 minutes, until softened. Add spinach and watercress and season with salt and pepper. Stirring often, cook just until spinach is wilted. Remove from the heat and set aside.

Combine whipping cream and water chestnuts in a medium pot on medium heat. Cook until cream is reduced by half, about 5 minutes. Stir in the wilted greens and mix until hot and well combined. Serve immediately. Refrigerate leftovers in an airtight container for up to 2 days.

4 cups chicken stock (page 155) or water

1¼ cups cornmeal

1 tsp sea salt

⅛ tsp black pepper

¼ cup unsalted butter

¼ cup freshly grated
Parmesan cheese

¼ cup mascarpone cheese
or softened cream cheese

AT HOME I make this side dish of fine Italian cornmeal at least once a month because it goes with so many things. An easy substitute for mashed potatoes, it is an ideal complement for braised lamb shank, osso buco (page 136) or braised short ribs (page 122). Stone-ground cornmeal has the most flavour, and a medium grind results in an appealing texture. Just before serving this polenta, add some additional grated cheese or dress it up with flavoured oils or herbs or garlic. Serves 6

CHEF'S TIP Store cornmeal in your freezer or refrigerator to retain freshness.

In a heavy-bottomed pan, bring chicken stock (or water) to a slow simmer on medium heat. Using a whisk, slowly pour cornmeal into the stock (or water) until smooth and well combined. Reduce the heat to as low as possible and cook, stirring occasionally with a wooden spoon, for 30 to 40 minutes. The cornmeal is cooked when it comes away from the sides of the pan. Stir in salt, black pepper, butter, Parmesan cheese and mascarpone (or cream) cheese and remove from the heat. The polenta should have the consistency of mashed potatoes. If the polenta is too thick, add more stock (or water). Serve immediately.

Will keep refrigerated in an airtight container for up to 3 days. Reheat cold polenta in a saucepan with ½ cup chicken stock (or water) on low heat, stirring constantly, until smooth and hot.

Kasha with Leeks
and Shiitake Mushrooms

1 cup whole buckwheat
kasha (not cracked)

1 tsp + 1 Tbsp extra-virgin olive oil

2 cups vegetable or
chicken stock (page 155)

1 sprig fresh thyme

⅛ tsp cayenne pepper

2 bay leaves

1 large leek, white and light green
parts only, cleaned and thinly sliced

12 shiitake mushrooms, cleaned and
stems discarded, tops thinly sliced

2 tsp tamari

MORE and more people are adding a variety of whole grains to their diets, and chefs are increasingly putting them on restaurant menus as well. My good friend Charlie Trotter was already using lesser-known grains like kasha on his vegetarian menus years ago, and he taught me just how versatile and flavourful they can be.

Kasha, also known as buckwheat groats, is a roasted grain with a nutty taste. Its bold flavour works well with greens such as steamed bok choy or sautéed kale cooked with garlic and olive oil. This side dish is great with fish or meat dishes or as a filling for zucchini, peppers, tomatoes or cabbage rolls. Serves 4 to 6

CHEF'S TIP When using leeks, discard the dark green tops, trim off the roots and slice lengthwise. Rinse carefully under running water—a lot of dirt can hide in between the layers right near the root. Pat dry and slice as needed.

Using a fine-mesh sieve, rinse kasha under cold running water. Drain well and transfer to a medium bowl. Stir in the 1 tsp olive oil and combine until grains are well coated, then transfer to a heavy-bottomed pot on medium heat. Stir constantly with a wooden spoon, breaking up lumps, until kasha is separated into individual grains. This step seals the kasha kernels so they do not become mushy during subsequent cooking.

Reduce the heat to low and add vegetable (or chicken) stock, thyme, cayenne and bay leaves. Cover and simmer for 20 to 25 minutes, or until all liquid is absorbed. Turn off the heat (the kasha will stay warm on the cooling burner while the leek mixture cooks). Remove and discard the thyme sprig and bay leaves.

Heat a medium nonstick frying pan on medium. Add leeks, mushrooms and tamari and sauté for about 5 minutes, stirring constantly, until vegetables soften a little. Remove from the heat.

Transfer cooked kasha to a large bowl. Stir in the leek and mushroom mixture and season with salt and black pepper. Drizzle with the 1 Tbsp extra-virgin olive oil and serve immediately. Refrigerate leftover kasha in an airtight container for up to 3 days.

Wild Rice **Pilaf**

1 cup wild rice

5 cups water

5 Tbsp extra-virgin olive oil

¼ cup diced onions

¼ cup diced carrots

¼ cup diced celery

¼ lb shiitake mushrooms, cleaned and stems discarded, in ¼-inch slices

1 tsp dried tarragon

1 Tbsp fresh lemon juice

1 tsp sea salt

½ tsp black pepper

⅓ lb snow peas, strings removed and cut in thirds

WILD RICE, which is actually a long-grain marsh grass, is expensive because the better-quality varieties are still harvested by hand. It's worth paying the price for its nutty flavour and versatility, however. Hot, this pilaf makes a perfect accompaniment to poultry of all kinds, including chicken pot pie (page 109), and to osso buco (page 136) or butterflied lamb (page 124). Cold, it makes a hearty salad when mixed with nuts and dried fruits—such as toasted almonds, pine nuts or pecans, with dried cranberries or sour cherries—and tossed with sherry vinaigrette (page 51). To save time, you can cook the rice the day before you plan to serve this pilaf. Serves 6

Place rice in a fine-mesh sieve and rinse under running water to remove any dirt or other impurities. Bring 3 cups of the water to a boil in a medium pot on high heat. Stir in rice and cook uncovered at a steady bubble for 20 minutes, stirring occasionally.

Remove from the heat and drain rice in a colander. The rice should be partially cooked, and still firm. Set aside. (If you are not using it immediately, allow rice to cool, then transfer to an airtight container and refrigerate for up to 3 days.)

Heat olive oil in a large saucepan on medium. Add onions, carrots and celery and sauté for about 5 minutes, stirring constantly, until onions are translucent. Add mushrooms and cook for another 2 to 3 minutes. Stir in wild rice, tarragon and the remaining 2 cups of water. Bring to a boil on medium-high heat, then reduce the heat to low and simmer, covered, for 15 minutes or until the liquid is evaporated. Add lemon juice and stir well. Stir in salt, black pepper and snow peas and cook, uncovered, for 3 to 4 minutes, stirring occasionally to prevent sticking. Remove from the heat while snow peas are still crisp and fresh in texture, and serve immediately. To store leftovers, remove snow peas, then refrigerate in an airtight container for up to 5 days.

Grainy Mustard **Spaetzle**

4 large eggs

3 Tbsp water

1 Tbsp vegetable oil

3 Tbsp grainy mustard

2 Tbsp melted unsalted butter
+ 2 Tbsp butter for sautéing

1½ cups all-purpose flour

½ tsp salt

⅛ tsp black pepper

SPAETZLE is a fun dish to make and, when done right, is one of the simplest pleasures in life. These little noodles remind me of the many trips to Germany and Austria I took in my early cooking days. There, this is a classic side dish served with game, but I love it with veal, chicken and beef as well. What I really like about this perfect starch is that it goes well with sauce of any kind and is also delicious as dumplings in soups and stews.

In this version I have added grainy mustard for added flavour and some zing, but you can vary the taste by using fresh herbs instead of mustard. The key to perfect spaetzle is adding the noodles once the butter starts to foam, and tossing them to give them a slightly golden look. Serves 6

Crack eggs into a large bowl and add water, vegetable oil, mustard and the 2 Tbsp melted butter. Mix well. Using a whisk, slowly incorporate flour a bit at a time, stirring constantly to prevent lumps. The texture should be like thick pancake batter. (If it is too thick, add water, 2 tsp at a time; if it is too thin, allow it to sit for 10 minutes.) Stir in salt and pepper.

Fill a large bowl with ice water. Fill a large pot with lightly salted water and set a stainless steel colander or ricer over it. Bring water to a boil on high heat.

Pour half the spaetzle batter into the colander (or ricer) set over the pot of boiling water. Using a rubber spatula, push the batter through the colander (or ricer). Small noodle-like shapes will form when the batter falls into the boiling water. Cook for 2 to 3 minutes, and when the noodles float to the top, use a slotted spoon to transfer them to the ice water. Repeat with the remaining batter. Once all the noodles are cooked, drain them in a colander and transfer to a large platter. (Cooked spaetzle can be patted dry and refrigerated in an airtight container for up to 3 days.)

To serve spaetzle, heat the remaining 2 Tbsp of butter in a large frying pan on medium heat. Allow butter to brown and begin to foam, about 2 minutes, then add spaetzle. Cook, tossing frequently, until lightly browned and hot, about 5 minutes. Season with salt and pepper to taste. Serve immediately.

POTATOES, GRAINS & PASTA

Poutine with Chorizo
and Dungeness Crab

Poutine gravy

1½ tsp vegetable oil

½ cup roughly chopped carrots

½ cup roughly chopped onions

½ cup roughly chopped celery

1 sprig fresh thyme

1 clove garlic, roughly chopped

6 whole black peppercorns

1 cup chicken stock (page 155)

½ cup veal stock (page 156)

2 tsp Worcestershire sauce

2 Tbsp ketchup

1 Tbsp unsalted butter

1 Tbsp all-purpose flour

¼ tsp salt

Poutine

2 lbs Yukon Gold potatoes

2 Tbsp extra-virgin olive oil

¼ lb fresh Dungeness crabmeat, cooked and picked over for cartilage

1 Tbsp fresh lemon juice

2 cups Cheddar cheese curds

¼ lb smoked chorizo sausages, casing removed, in ¼-inch angled slices

1 cup poutine gravy, hot

At FEENIE'S, I was famous for a poutine made with crab, lobster and short rib meat. Poutine is a staple food in Quebec, and I put it on the menu when I opened the restaurant because I had so many French Canadians working for me! At that time, I ate either a Feenie Burger or a Feenie Weenie with this poutine once a week. I don't do that anymore, but I still miss the gravy. It's also a great cure for hangovers.

This version is an indulgent dish that's worth the money for the crab and the time you put into making it. You can use homemade fries, as we have shown you here, or substitute store-bought ones if you're pressed for time. Be sure to serve the poutine on warm plates. Serves 4

Poutine gravy Heat a large pot on medium and add vegetable oil. Stir in carrots, onions and celery and sauté until soft and caramelized, stirring frequently, 10 to 15 minutes. Add thyme, garlic and peppercorns, then pour in chicken and veal stocks, Worcestershire sauce and ketchup. Bring the mixture to a boil, reduce the heat to medium-low and simmer for about 15 minutes to extract flavour from the vegetables.

In a separate small pot, melt butter on medium heat. Using a whisk, slowly incorporate flour and cook for 1 to 2 minutes to make a roux. *Continued overleaf >*

69

Add a ladleful of the hot gravy mixture to the roux, whisking constantly to prevent lumps from forming. Slowly pour this thickened mixture back into the rest, stirring constantly with a wooden spoon to mix well. Continue stirring the thickening gravy until flour is completely cooked and the gravy coats the back of a spoon, about 5 minutes. Season very lightly with salt, then strain the mixture through a fine-mesh sieve. Discard the solids.

If you are not using the gravy right away, allow to cool and then refrigerate in an airtight container for up to 4 days.

Poutine Preheat the oven to 400°F.

Peel potatoes and use a very sharp knife to cut them into French fries ½ inch wide and 4 or 5 inches long. Spread fries on a baking sheet and toss with olive oil, then arrange them in a single layer. Bake, shaking the pan and turning fries over occasionally, until golden brown and tender, about 25 minutes. Remove from the oven, season with salt and pepper and set aside. Reduce the oven temperature to 375°F.

In a small bowl, gently combine crabmeat with lemon juice and add salt and pepper to taste. Set aside.

In an ovenproof dish, arrange half of the fries in a single layer. Top with half of the cheese curds and all of the chorizo. Repeat with another layer of fries, the remaining cheese curds and the crabmeat. Bake for 5 to 7 minutes, until cheese curds just start to melt. Remove from the oven immediately or the cheese curds will become tough.

Divide poutine among 4 plates, top with gravy and serve immediately.

1 cup quinoa, washed well and drained

1½ cups vegetable stock

1 Tbsp extra-virgin olive oil
or vegetable stock

1 medium onion,
in ¼-inch dice (about 1 cup)

1 red or yellow bell pepper,
in ¼-inch dice (about 1 cup)

1 medium zucchini,
in ¼-inch dice (about 1 cup)

2 cups peeled eggplant, in ¼-inch dice

10 to 12 crimini mushrooms, sliced

1 rib celery, in ¼-inch dice

5 cloves garlic, minced

1 to 2 tsp crushed chili flakes

1 (28-oz) tin good-quality
crushed tomatoes

¼ cup chopped fresh parsley

1 Tbsp chopped fresh thyme

HERE is another great quinoa dish for vegetarians. This jambalaya is tasty, good for you and very versatile. It is also forgiving, and can be a good, quick way to sneak lots of vegetables (or surplus bounty from the garden) into one dish. Try it as a light lunch or as a side dish with fish. Serves 6

In a medium pot, combine quinoa and the 1½ cups vegetable stock and bring to a simmer on medium heat. Cover, reduce the heat to low and cook until all the liquid is absorbed, 15 to 20 minutes. Set aside.

In a large pot, heat olive oil (or vegetable stock) on medium. Add onions and sauté for 2 minutes, or until translucent. Stirring constantly, add bell peppers, zucchini, eggplant, mushrooms, celery, garlic and chili flakes and cook for 5 minutes. Pour in tomatoes and cook for another 10 minutes, until eggplant is soft.

Just before serving, gently fold quinoa, parsley and thyme into the vegetable mixture. Transfer to a large bowl and serve, family-style. Leftovers will keep refrigerated in an airtight container for up to 2 days.

Crab **Crêpes**

Crêpes

¾ cup all-purpose flour

⅛ tsp salt

2 large eggs, beaten

1 cup whole milk, cold

1 Tbsp melted unsalted butter

1 tsp vegetable oil

Crab filling

1 Tbsp unsalted butter

⅓ cup chopped green onions

½ cup sliced fresh mushrooms

½ tsp dried thyme OR
1 tsp chopped fresh thyme

1½ tsp all-purpose flour

¼ cup + 2 Tbsp whole milk

2 Tbsp dry white wine

½ lb fresh Dungeness crabmeat,
cooked and picked over for cartilage

1 Tbsp chopped fresh parsley

1½ tsp fresh lemon juice

½ Tbsp Dijon mustard

⅛ tsp salt

½ tsp chili flakes

2 tsp cold butter,
for greasing the pan

WHO does not love crêpes? Virtually every country in the world makes something like them—sometimes filled, sometimes topped with various condiments. I first started making them in elementary school as an after-school snack at my friend Pat's house. We covered them in sugar. Later, during my travels to Brittany, I tried savoury crêpes and I eventually ended up making them every day during my first job at Bistro de Paris in Vancouver. These days, one of my favourite things to do with my kids, besides baking pizza, is making crêpes.

This crêpe recipe works well with both sweet and savoury fillings. It can be a very fast meal if you cover the crêpes in maple syrup, or serve them with jam, or lemon juice and sugar, or Nutella. Or you can put together a more complex stuffed variation, such as a roasted fruit or vegetable + soft cheese (or soft spread like hummus or eggplant caviar) + fresh herbs, or béchamel + ragout, or berries + crème Chantilly.

A good crêpe is wafer thin with a lacy edge and is made in a classic crêpe pan. That pan is six to eight inches in diameter and has fairly shallow sides to make turning the crêpes easier, but a cast-iron, nonstick or stainless steel frying pan will also work well. The side that's cooked first is called the "right" side and is more attractive, so place the filling on the other side. Serves 4 to 6

Crêpes In a medium bowl, combine flour and salt. Using a whisk, add eggs and beat until smooth. Very gradually add milk, whisking constantly to prevent lumps from forming. Stir in butter and beat until the batter is smooth. Refrigerate, covered, for at least 2 hours or for up to 2 days. (Crêpe batter thickens on standing.)

Remove crêpe batter from the refrigerator. If necessary, add water or milk until it has the consistency of light cream. Place a kitchen towel on a clean work surface.

Brush the bottom of a nonstick or classic crêpe pan with ⅛ tsp of vegetable oil and heat on medium. Using a ladle, pour about 3 Tbsp of batter into the pan. Quickly tilt the pan in all directions so the batter covers the pan in a thin film. Cook for 1 minute. With a plastic lifter, lift the edge of the crêpe to test for doneness. The crêpe is ready for flipping when it is golden and can be shaken loose from the pan. (The first crêpe is sometimes too oily or torn to fill; it has "conditioned" the pan for the following crêpes and can just be eaten on its own.) Flip crêpe and cook for 30 seconds. Transfer to the kitchen towel and allow to cool. Repeat with the remaining batter, brushing the pan with ⅛ tsp of oil, if necessary, between every 2 or 3 crêpes. You should have 12 crêpes when done.

Cooled cooked crêpes keep well when refrigerated. Cut twelve 6-inch squares of waxed paper. Place one crêpe in an airtight container, cover with a sheet of waxed paper and place another crêpe on top. Continue stacking crêpes in this manner, then refrigerate for up to 2 days.

Crab filling Place the 1 Tbsp butter in a medium pot on medium heat. Add green onions, mushrooms and thyme and cook, stirring occasionally, until tender, 6 to 8 minutes. Reduce the heat to low and add flour. Cook for 1 minute, stirring constantly. Gradually add milk and white wine, increase the heat to medium and cook, stirring constantly, until thickened. Remove from the heat and stir in crabmeat, parsley, lemon juice, mustard, salt and chili flakes.

Preheat the oven to 350°F. Lightly grease an ovenproof baking pan.

Finish crêpes Arrange crêpes on a clean work surface. Spoon 2 Tbsp of the crabmeat mixture in a 3-inch horizontal line about 1 inch from the bottom edge of each crêpe. Fold the bottom edge of the crêpe over the filling, tuck in the sides and continue rolling to create tight cylinders that completely encase the filling. Arrange rolled crêpes, seam side down, in a single layer in the baking pan and bake for 20 minutes. Turn the broiler on and brown the top of the crêpes, watching carefully (this will take about 1 minute). Serve hot.

Paella with Chorizo,
Chicken and Seafood

¼ cup extra-virgin olive oil

½ lb chorizo sausage, in ¼-inch slices

2 cloves garlic, minced

1 boneless and skinless
chicken breast, 6 oz, in 1-inch dice

1 lb raw, unpeeled prawns

½ lb halibut fillets, in strips 1 inch wide

½ lb cleaned squid tubes
and tentacles, in ½-inch rings

1 onion, finely chopped

2 cups short-grain rice

3½ cups chicken stock (page 155)

Large pinch of saffron threads

½ lb live mussels, scrubbed
clean and beards removed

½ tomato, peeled, seeded and
cut in ¼-inch dice (about ½ cup)

A TRADITIONAL dish in Spanish cooking, paella is also the name of the pan it's cooked in. The two-handled pans vary in diameter but are typically thirteen, fourteen or sixteen inches across and usually only a couple of inches deep. A sixteen-inch paella pan or a large shallow flameproof casserole dish or a large cast-iron frying pan will work well for this recipe.

When the flavours are balanced, paella is a soothing comfort food. Ingredients vary from region to region but all are based on saffron-flavoured rice. This version is a twist on a dish prepared for me by a local chef in the Rioja countryside. It was made with ease and simplicity and, of course, with some good local wine. This remains a dish I must prepare at least a few times a year. Serves 6 to 8

Heat 2 Tbsp of the olive oil in a paella pan on medium-high heat. Add chorizo and 1 tsp of the minced garlic and cook for 2 minutes. Use a slotted spoon to transfer chorizo to a large plate. If the pan is dry, heat 2 tsp olive oil. Add chicken and cook for 3 minutes. Transfer to the plate with the chorizo. If the pan is dry, add 2 tsp more olive oil before cooking each ingredient. Add prawns and cook until shells are pink, about 2 minutes. Transfer to the plate. Next, quickly sear halibut on all sides for about 2 minutes total. Transfer to the plate. Finally, quickly sear squid on all sides, about 2 minutes total. Transfer to the plate. Set aside all the cooked ingredients.

Add another 2 Tbsp of the oil to the paella pan. Add onions and the remaining garlic and sauté, stirring occasionally, until onions are translucent, about 5 minutes. Add rice and stir, coating each grain with oil. Pour in chicken stock and bring the liquid to a boil. Add saffron and continue to boil stock fairly rapidly, stirring occasionally, until some of the liquid has been absorbed and rice is cloudy but still firm, 15 minutes.

Place chorizo, chicken, prawns, halibut, squid and mussels on top of rice and do not stir. Cover with a lid or heavy aluminum foil and cook for another 5 minutes. Add tomato, reduce the heat to low and allow flavours to infuse for 10 more minutes before serving. (If the liquid evaporates before the rice is cooked, add more stock or water, 2 Tbsp at a time.) Discard any mussels that do not open and serve immediately.

Fettuccine *with Clams*

in White Wine and Parsley Sauce

¾ pkg (12 oz/340 g) fettuccine

2 Tbsp extra-virgin olive oil

2 Tbsp unsalted butter

2 oz thinly sliced pancetta,
in ¼-inch strips

3 cloves garlic, minced

½ tsp chili flakes

⅓ cup chopped fresh parsley

½ cup fish stock (page 154) or clam nectar

½ cup dry white wine

2 lb live Manila or littleneck clams,
scrubbed clean and rinsed well
in cold running water

1 tsp salt

½ tsp black pepper

WHEN I started at Cactus Club Restaurants in 2008, my co-worker Christy Murphy challenged me to an Iron Chef competition. Apparently her father, Lorne Wilson, makes "the best-ever" *pasta alle vongole*. In our competition, Christy used canned clams and, surprisingly, didn't win. We had good fun, though. Try this version, Lorne Wilson! This recipe is much better: one important trick is the low amount of liquid I use, as you never want to drown the pasta in sauce. Serve this pasta in warmed bowls.

CHEF'S TIP Inspect all clams before using them. Discard any that are open and won't close when their shells are tapped. And if time permits, soak the clams in cold water for a few hours before rinsing them. Otherwise, rinse them repeatedly in fresh changes of water, or set them under a continuous stream of cold water, until any water coming off them is clear. Serves 4

Bring a large pot of salted water to a boil on high heat. Add fettuccine and cook for 2 minutes less than the time on the package directions. Drain pasta well in a colander, toss with 1 tsp of the olive oil and set aside.

In a large heavy frying pan, melt butter on medium-high heat. Add pancetta and cook, stirring often, until golden, about 3 minutes. Transfer pancetta to a small bowl.

Drain off all but about 1 Tbsp of fat from the pan. Add garlic, chili flakes and 2 Tbsp of the parsley and stir for 1 minute. Pour in fish stock (or clam nectar) and white wine and bring to a boil. Add clams. Cover and cook until they open, about 5 minutes. Discard any clams that do not open. Add pancetta and pasta, stirring to heat pasta and coat it well with the sauce. Add salt, pepper and the remaining parsley and toss well.

Divide pasta among 4 bowls, ensuring that the sauce and clams are evenly distributed. Finish each serving with a drizzle of olive oil. Serve immediately.

Spaghetti with Spicy Chicken
and Chanterelle Mushrooms

3 Tbsp salt

1 pkg (16 oz/500 g) spaghetti

½ cup + 2 tsp extra-virgin olive oil

10 oz ground chicken

1 tsp chili flakes

1 tsp minced garlic

4 oz chanterelle mushrooms, brushed clean, large pieces cut in half

1 cup roughly diced fresh tomatoes (1 large)

2 Tbsp finely chopped fresh flat-leaf parsley

THIS pasta is one of our family favourites because it's simple to make and has so much flavour. Although my kids and I like it spicy, just back off on the chili flakes if you do not. It is also a dry pasta, but add a bit of pasta water if you need more moisture.

Try to make this pasta in the fall when juicy tomatoes and fresh nutty-flavoured chanterelles are abundant in the markets. Out of season, use the same quantity of crimini mushrooms plus a few crushed, dried chanterelles. Serve this pasta in warm bowls. Serves 4 to 6

Bring a large pot of water and the 3 Tbsp salt to a boil on high heat. Add spaghetti and cook, stirring occasionally, for 2 minutes less than the time on the package directions, or until al dente. Pour 1 cup of the pasta cooking water into a small bowl, then drain pasta in a colander. Toss pasta with the 2 tsp olive oil and set aside.

Heat a large frying pan on medium-high and add the ½ cup olive oil. Sprinkle a large pinch of salt over oil to prevent chicken from sticking to the pan. Add chicken and cook for 2 minutes, stirring constantly and breaking chicken into small pieces. Add chili flakes and garlic and cook for 1 minute. Stir in chanterelles and cook for 2 to 3 minutes, until mushrooms are soft. Add tomatoes and parsley and cook for another 5 minutes. If necessary, thin the sauce with some of the reserved pasta water. Season sauce with salt and freshly ground black pepper.

Add pasta to the frying pan, tossing well with the sauce until everything is combined and heated through. Serve in warm bowls.

Rigatoni with Braised Lamb
and Chanterelle Mushrooms

Braised lamb

4 lamb shanks, each 10 to 14 oz

2 Tbsp extra-virgin olive oil

2 cups dry white wine

5 to 6 shallots, peeled and cut in half

2 to 3 whole garlic cloves, peeled

2 to 3 sprigs fresh thyme

Roasted garlic

½ cup whole garlic cloves, unpeeled

1 Tbsp extra-virgin olive oil

½ tsp fresh thyme

As you may already know by now, I love pasta. For inspiring this recipe, I thank Pino Posteraro, at whose home I had one of the best pastas ever with his wife and children. He did not share all the details, as I'm sure the recipe is a family secret, but he gave me enough that I can share some of the flavours with you.

This recipe also reminds me of Sweden, where I picked fifty pounds of chanterelles in one day. It was the first wild product I had ever harvested in my life, and I have never forgotten that day. The best way to clean chanterelle mushrooms is to use a small paring knife to gently scrape the dirt off or a clean pastry brush to lightly brush the mushrooms. Do not wash the mushrooms in water because this washes away the distinctive chanterelle flavour and changes the texture slightly. Serves 6 to 8

Braised lamb Preheat the oven to 325°F. Season lamb shanks with salt and freshly ground black pepper.

Place a large ovenproof pan on high heat and pour in olive oil. When oil is hot, add lamb shanks and sear for about 1 minute on each side. Deglaze the pan with white wine, stirring up any brown bits on the bottom of the pan. Add shallots, garlic and thyme. Cover the pan, place it in the oven and cook for 2½ to 3 hours, or until meat is falling off the bone. Remove from the oven and allow to cool briefly. Reserving the braising liquid, use your hands to transfer the meat to a large bowl.

Chanterelle mushroom rigatoni

1 pkg (16 oz/500 g) rigatoni	1 lb chanterelle mushrooms, cleaned
2 Tbsp extra-virgin olive oil	¼ cup roasted whole garlic cloves
4 Tbsp chopped shallots	4 cups shredded braised lamb
1 tsp freshly chopped garlic	1 cup lamb braising liquid
	1 Tbsp chopped fresh parsley
	2 cups baby arugula
	2 tsp white truffle oil

Strain the still-warm braising liquid through a fine-mesh sieve into a clean bowl. Using a spoon, skim and discard any fat from the surface. Set aside.

Shred the meat roughly with a fork, being sure to break up any large chunks into 1 to 1½-inch pieces. Discard any bones, fat and cartilage. You should have about 4 cups of shredded lamb. Set aside.

Roasted garlic Preheat the oven to 375°F. Line a baking sheet with parchment paper. Trim garlic cloves at both ends to remove the hard root and tip bits. In a small bowl, toss garlic with olive oil and thyme. Arrange on the baking sheet and roast for 15 to 20 minutes until soft and evenly brown. Allow garlic to cool, then peel and discard the skins. Set flesh aside in a small bowl.

Chanterelle mushroom rigatoni Bring a large pot of salted water to a boil on high heat. Add pasta and cook 2 minutes less than the directions on the package, or until al dente. Drain in a colander and set aside.

Heat a large frying pan on medium and add olive oil. Stir in shallots and sauté until translucent, 2 to 3 minutes. Add chopped garlic, sauté slightly, then stir in mushrooms and cook for 3 to 4 minutes, until soft. They will release an intense mushroom aroma.

Add roasted garlic, shredded lamb and lamb braising liquid and cook for another minute. Stir in parsley, then add pasta and toss well. Season with salt and black pepper to taste. Add baby arugula and stir gently. Drizzle with truffle oil. Toss once and serve immediately.

Butternut Squash and
Fava Bean Farfalle

with Brown Butter and Sage Sauce

3 Tbsp extra-virgin olive oil

1 pkg (16 oz/500 g) whole wheat farfalle

1 butternut squash, about 2 lbs

¼ cup unsalted butter

1 large sweet onion (red or white Spanish), in ½-inch dice

10 fresh sage leaves

2 cloves garlic, minced

1 tsp salt

1 cup cooked fava beans

⅛ tsp freshly ground black pepper

½ cup freshly grated Parmesan cheese

OVER the years, butternut squash ravioli has become one of my signature dishes, first at Lumière and Feenie's, now at Cactus Club Cafe. I love butternut squash for the sheer simplicity of its flavour and the fact that it tastes great with pasta. In this simple recipe, we pair it with farfalle, or bow-tie pasta, which has the perfect shape to hold chunky vegetable sauces such as this one, as well as brown butter and sage. Pappardelle and fettuccine are other good pasta shapes to use. And you can use another winter squash or a pumpkin in this recipe if you do not have any butternut squash.

The key to this dish is to keep the heat on medium-low so as not to burn the butter. And though it is a great winter dish, try it in the summer as well, when you could grill the squash on the barbecue. Warm the bowls before serving this pasta and garnish with toasted pine nuts or crumbled amaretti biscuits. Serves 6

Preheat the oven to 375°F.

Using a long heavy knife, cut squash in half lengthwise. Peel and discard the skin. Using a melon baller, scoop out the seeds and discard them. Cut squash in 1-inch cubes and place in a large bowl. Add onions, salt and black pepper and mix well. Add olive oil and toss to coat. Arrange the squash and onion mixture on a baking sheet large enough to hold it all in a single layer. Roast for 30 minutes, or until tender and lightly browned.

Heat a large pot of salted water on high heat. Add pasta and cook for 2 minutes less than the time on the package directions. Pour 1 cup of the pasta cooking water into a small bowl, then drain pasta in a colander. (If you are not using it immediately, allow pasta to cool, toss it with 2 tsp olive oil, then transfer to an airtight container and refrigerate for up to 1 day.) Set aside.

In a large frying pan, heat butter and sage on medium-low until butter begins to brown, about 2 minutes. When the sediment becomes medium brown, add garlic and continue cooking for 1 minute. Remove the pan from the heat to prevent garlic from burning.

Remove sage with a slotted spoon, crumble it and return it to the pan. Add pasta, fava beans and the squash and onion mixture and toss well. Return the pan to the heat (on medium-low) and warm through. If necessary, thin the sauce with some of the reserved pasta water. Season with salt and black pepper.

Divide the pasta among warm bowls and top with Parmesan cheese. Serve immediately. Will keep refrigerated in an airtight container for up to 2 days.

Lobster **Mac 'n' Cheese**

Béchamel sauce

4 cups whole milk

2 cloves garlic, peeled and crushed

¼ cup unsalted butter

¼ cup all-purpose flour

Pinch of freshly grated nutmeg

Freshly ground white pepper

Lobster mac 'n' cheese

1 live lobster, about 1 lb

2 tsp vegetable oil

8 oz Irish or double-smoked bacon, in ¼-inch dice

4 shallots, peeled and finely chopped

¼ cup grated Emmental cheese

¼ cup crumbled blue cheese

¼ cup grated sharp white Cheddar cheese

½ cup freshly grated Pecorino Romano cheese

16 oz gnocchi (page 165), cooked (about 3 cups loosely filled)

DESPITE its name, this is not really your traditional macaroni and cheese but a decadent mix of gnocchi, four cheeses and lobster. What's such a treat about this dish is that if you're going to be indulgent, you might as well go over the top. You can add fresh raw scallops or spot prawns poached in boiling salted water (add a quarter cup of white wine and one chopped shallot) for two to three minutes, as well as smoked salmon. I've used my favourite cheeses here, but you could vary them if you want. Serves 4 to 6

CHEF'S TIP Kitchen scissors can help to remove the meat from the lobster tail. Make a straight cut on both sides of the tail under the hard shell and peel it back, then extract the lobster meat with a small fork.

Béchamel sauce Combine milk and garlic in a medium pot on medium heat. Bring to a boil and remove from the heat. Cover and allow to infuse for 10 minutes. Strain through a fine-mesh strainer and discard the solids.

Make a roux by melting butter in a heavy-bottomed pot on medium heat. Whisk in flour and cook for about 1 minute, or until light brown. Remove from the heat and allow to cool slightly, 30 seconds to 1 minute.

Add strained hot milk, whisking constantly, to the roux. Return the pot to medium heat and bring the mixture back to a boil, whisking constantly until the sauce thickens. Add nutmeg, then season to taste with salt and freshly ground white pepper. Allow the sauce to simmer for 3 more minutes. Remove from the heat. Place a piece of plastic wrap directly on the surface of the sauce and set aside. (This step prevents a skin from forming on top of the sauce.)

Lobster mac 'n' cheese Bring a large pot of salted water to a boil on high heat and add lobster. Cook for 3 minutes at a rolling boil. Using tongs, remove lobster from the water, place on a clean work surface and allow to cool. Using kitchen scissors, a small hammer and a small fork, crack shells and remove lobster meat from the tail and claws. Discard shells and cut meat in ¾-inch dice. Set aside.

Preheat the oven to 375°F. Have four to six 3-cup casserole dishes (or one 9- × 12-inch glass or ceramic baking dish) ready. Line 4 to 6 plates (or one large platter) with napkins.

Line a small bowl with a paper towel. Heat vegetable oil in a small frying pan on medium-high. Add bacon and shallots and sauté for about 5 minutes, or until bacon is just cooked and shallots are translucent. Using a slotted spoon, transfer the mixture to the lined bowl and set aside.

Remove the plastic wrap from the béchamel sauce and reheat on medium-low. Whisk in Emmental, blue cheese, Cheddar and half of the Pecorino Romano. Add half of the bacon-shallot mixture and fold in lobster meat.

Divide gnocchi among casserole dishes (or arrange it in the bottom of the baking dish) and cover with enough sauce to top pasta by half an inch. Sprinkle with the remaining Pecorino Romano and the remaining bacon-shallot mixture. Bake for 15 to 20 minutes, or until hot and bubbling.

Turn the broiler on. Watching closely, leave mac 'n' cheese under the broiler for 3 to 5 minutes, or until the top is light golden brown. Set each casserole dish (or the baking dish) on a napkin-lined plate. Serve immediately.

Butternut Squash and
Ricotta Gnocchi

with Tomato and Basil Sauce

Butternut squash purée

1 butternut squash, about 2 lbs

Butternut squash and ricotta gnocchi

1½ cups raw milk ricotta cheese

1½ cups butternut squash purée

3 large egg yolks

1½ tsp salt

½ cup all-purpose flour

1½ cups tomato and
basil sauce (page 161), hot

½ cup freshly grated Parmesan cheese

1½ tsp extra-virgin olive oil

MY SON describes these gnocchi as being as light as pillows, and it's one of my favourite recipes because of this delicate texture. Served with the simple tomato sauce, this dish reminds me of Italy. I could eat it all year long.

Begin making the gnocchi the day before you plan to serve them. And be careful when handling the gnocchi, as they are very delicate. Add a touch more flour if you find them too difficult to work with. Serves 6

Butternut squash purée Preheat the oven to 375°F. Line a baking sheet with parchment paper.

Cut squash in half lengthwise and place on the baking sheet, cut sides down. Bake until squash is soft and lightly coloured, about 30 minutes. Allow to cool slightly, about 10 minutes, then remove and discard skins. In a medium bowl, mash the squash with a fork or a potato masher until it becomes a smooth purée. Cover and refrigerate until chilled.

Butternut squash and ricotta gnocchi Position a sieve over a large bowl or line the bowl with two layers of cheesecloth, making sure the cheesecloth hangs above the bottom of the bowl to allow excess liquid to drain. Set ricotta cheese in the sieve or cheesecloth, cover with plastic wrap and refrigerate at least 4 hours, or preferably overnight. Discard liquid from the ricotta.

Place ricotta, chilled squash purée, egg yolks and salt in a large bowl. Using a spatula, gently fold ingredients together until combined. Very gently fold in flour until well mixed. Form into a ball, cover with plastic wrap and refrigerate for at least 1 hour, so the gluten in the flour can expand and the dough firm up.

Line a baking sheet with parchment paper. Lightly sprinkle a clean, dry work surface with flour. Cut dough into quarters, then gently roll each quarter into a cylinder 1 inch in diameter. Using a plastic pastry cutter or a small knife, cut each cylinder into 1-inch pieces, pinching the ends of each piece to round them slightly. Arrange gnocchi in a single layer on the baking sheet and set in the freezer for up to 2 hours to firm up.

To cook, bring a large pot of salted water to a gentle boil on medium-low heat. Gently drop gnocchi, in batches, into the pot and cook for 2 to 3 minutes, or until they float to the surface of the pot. Using a slotted spoon, transfer cooked gnocchi to a serving platter. Spoon tomato sauce overtop and sprinkle with Parmesan cheese. Drizzle with olive oil.

FISH & SHELLFISH

Poached Halibut
with Basil Vinaigrette

Basil vinaigrette

2 Tbsp Dijon mustard

2 Tbsp capers, rinsed

2 Tbsp chopped fresh flat-leaf parsley

4 Tbsp chopped or torn fresh basil

1 Tbsp sherry vinegar

1 Tbsp fresh lemon juice

½ tsp salt

¼ tsp black pepper

1 cup extra-virgin olive oil

Poached halibut

6 halibut fillets, each 6 oz, skin removed

3 Tbsp white vinegar

½ cup diced onions

½ cup diced carrots

½ cup diced celery

5 sprigs fresh flat-leaf parsley

1 sprig fresh thyme

6 whole black peppercorns

2 tsp salt

¾ cup basil vinaigrette, warmed

SIMPLE, simple, simple is always the way to go with fish, and this recipe is no exception. Here we poach the fish to keep it moist and tender and serve it with the most delicious basil vinaigrette. This is a quick summer meal that works well with cod, or you can substitute arctic char, if you prefer. Serve it with a side of wild rice pilaf (page 64) or with the spinach, bacon and blue cheese salad (page 48). Serves 6

Basil vinaigrette In a food processor, mix mustard, capers, parsley, basil, sherry vinegar, lemon juice, salt and pepper and pulse until well combined. With the motor running, slowly add olive oil in a thin stream until the mixture is emulsified. Will keep refrigerated in an airtight container for up to 1 week.

Poached halibut Place the fillets in a large, shallow pan and add enough water to come ¾ of the way up the halibut at its thickest part. Add white vinegar, onions, carrots, celery, parsley, thyme, peppercorns and salt. Bring to a gentle simmer on medium heat. Cook for 3 minutes (slightly longer if fillets are very thick). With a slotted spoon, transfer halibut to a large plate. Discard the poaching liquid.

Serve warm halibut on individual plates, drizzled with 2 Tbsp vinaigrette per serving.

Pan-Seared
Halibut with Morels

Morel Sauce

1 Tbsp unsalted butter

2 Tbsp extra-virgin olive oil

1 tsp chopped Thai red chili

1 clove garlic, minced

4 cups morel mushrooms, cleaned

½ tsp salt

⅛ tsp freshly ground black pepper

1 cup mushroom stock or chicken stock (page 155)

1 cup pearl onions, blanched and peeled

2 cups thin green beans, trimmed, blanched for 3 to 4 minutes, in 2-inch pieces

Halibut

4 halibut fillets, each 6 oz, skin removed

2 Tbsp extra-virgin olive oil

1 Tbsp unsalted butter

Grated rind of ½ lemon

1 tsp fresh thyme

THIS is a recipe I first made years ago and it is still one of my favourites, as the mushroom sauce has great flavour and helps keep the halibut moist. Halibut is a very versatile fish but it is prone to overcooking so it's best cooked gently in some liquid, as in this recipe. In the spring I like to use morels, but in other seasons, when they are not available, this dish works well with basic crimini mushrooms or chanterelles and even pine mushrooms. Serve the halibut on warm plates. **Serves 4**

Morel sauce Add butter, olive oil, chilies and garlic to a large frying pan on medium-high heat. Sauté for 1 minute, then add morels and season with salt and pepper. Sauté, stirring occasionally, until mushrooms are cooked, about 10 minutes. (The morels will release their liquid, which will evaporate as they continue to cook, concentrating their flavour.)

Add mushroom (or chicken) stock and pearl onions and bring to a boil. Reduce the heat to medium and cook until liquid is reduced to about ¼ cup and onions are tender, about 10 minutes. While sauce is reducing, cook halibut.

Halibut Season both sides of halibut fillets with a pinch of sea salt and freshly ground black or white pepper. Heat olive oil in a large frying pan on high heat. Reduce the heat to medium-high and add halibut. Sear until golden brown, about 2 minutes. Carefully turn fish over and add butter, lemon rind and thyme to the pan. Cook the halibut, basting it constantly with the pan juices, until flesh resists slightly when pressed gently with your fingertip, a further 2 to 4 minutes depending on the thickness of the fillets. Remove halibut from the heat and allow to rest for 3 to 4 minutes. While fish is resting, finish the sauce.

Finish morel sauce Add green beans to the reduced sauce and heat until they are just tender, 3 to 4 minutes. Place one piece of halibut on each plate and top with the morel sauce.

Marinated Barbecued
Steelhead Salmon

with Grilled Red Pepper and Corn Hash

Grilled red pepper and corn hash

2 Tbsp extra-virgin olive oil

2 Tbsp finely diced red onions

2 tsp minced garlic

2 grilled red bell peppers, in ½-inch dice (page 7)

2 grilled tomatillos, diced (page 7)

2 ears corn, kernels removed

2 jalapeño peppers, cut in half lengthwise and seeds discarded, finely chopped

2 tsp lime zest

2 Tbsp fresh lemon juice

½ cup chopped cilantro

2 tsp mustard seeds

1 tsp salt

½ tsp black pepper

Marinated barbecued salmon

2 Tbsp extra-virgin olive oil

2 Tbsp fresh lime juice

2 tsp lime zest

2 tsp chopped garlic

2 Tbsp chopped cilantro

1 tsp ground cumin

1 tsp chili powder

1 tsp salt

½ tsp black pepper

1 large steelhead salmon fillet, about 1½ lbs, skin on and pin bones removed

I LOVE summer barbecues, and this salmon dinner is one of my kids' and my wife's favourites. It's quick and easy to prepare, economical and very good for you, and now that steelhead salmon are available across Canada all year long, you can have this dish summer or winter. Here in B.C., we are fortunate to have one of the best fish farms in the world up at Lois Lake in Powell River. It has some of the most sound fish-farming practices I have ever seen, and by the time the salmon hits your table it has been out of the lake no more than three days. Now that is fresh.

My wife, Michelle, is a great cook, and she does a better job than I do of keeping this dish simple. We serve it with the bell pepper and corn mixture, which can be presented cold and fresh like a salsa or cooked like a hash. If serving cold like a salsa, you will want to blanch the corn beforehand. Place the ears of corn in a pot of boiling, salted water for two to three minutes. Drain the corn, allow to cool slightly, then cut off the kernels, discarding the cobs. In a medium bowl, combine the corn kernels with the other ingredients and allow the flavours to infuse for fifteen minutes. You can also serve this versatile hash with other fish or meats, as a salsa on sandwiches or as a dip with chips or vegetables. **Serves 4** *Continued overleaf >*

Grilled red pepper and corn hash Heat a frying pan on medium-high and add olive oil. When oil is hot, add onions and sauté until translucent, 5 to 6 minutes. Add garlic and cook for 2 minutes until fragrant. Stir in bell peppers and tomatillos and mix well. Reduce the heat to medium and stir in corn kernels, jalapeños, lime zest, lemon juice, cilantro, mustard seeds, salt and pepper. Cook for 3 to 5 minutes to allow the flavours to combine. The hash will keep refrigerated in an airtight container for up to 2 days.

Marinated barbecued salmon In a small bowl, combine olive oil, lime juice, lime zest, garlic, cilantro, cumin, chili powder, salt and pepper and mix thoroughly.

Place salmon, skin side down, in a roasting pan and pour the marinade overtop. Set aside to marinate at room temperature for 30 minutes.

Preheat the barbecue to 400°F. Remove salmon from the marinade and place skin side down on the barbecue. Brush with any marinade remaining in the pan, then grill for 7 to 8 minutes, uncovered and without turning fish over, until medium rare or to taste. The fish is cooked when it resists slightly when touched with your fingertip.

Transfer salmon, skin side down, to a warm platter. Allow it to rest for 5 minutes. Top with 2 to 3 Tbsp of the red pepper and corn hash and spoon the remaining hash into a serving bowl to pass at the table. Serve family-style, allowing guests to help themselves.

Citrus-cured steelhead salmon

Zest of 2 lemons

Zest of 2 limes

Zest of 2 oranges

¾ cup coarse salt

½ cup granulated sugar

1 large steelhead salmon fillet, about 1½ lbs, skin on and pin bones removed

1 Tbsp micro or very finely chopped cilantro

2 tsp fresh lemon juice

½ tsp Maldon salt

Horseradish-mustard vinaigrette

1 Tbsp grainy mustard

2 Tbsp Dijon mustard

5 Tbsp red wine vinegar

5 Tbsp horseradish

1 Tbsp fresh lemon juice

2 tsp honey

1 cup sunflower or canola oil

Warm potato salad

Pinch of saffron

1 cup boiling water

1 lb baby white nugget potatoes

2 tsp extra-virgin olive oil

Dijon dill mayonnaise

1 cup basic mayonnaise (page 158)

1 Tbsp chopped fresh dill

1 Tbsp Dijon mustard

I LIVED in Sweden when I was sixteen and it was one of the best years of my life. The country has some fantastic very fresh and very simple food, and that may be one of the reasons I wanted to become a chef. Classic gravlax is thinly sliced raw fish preserved like the Vikings did in a simple salt cure. My version uses local steelhead salmon in a quick salt, sugar and citrus cure. Serve it slightly warm with a matching warm potato salad. If you get the temperatures right, this will be one of the best first courses you will ever serve. **Serves 4 to 6**

Citrus-cured steelhead salmon In a medium bowl, combine lemon, lime and orange zests with coarse salt and sugar until thoroughly mixed.

Place salmon, flesh side up, in a large glass or stainless steel roasting pan. Coat flesh with the cure mixture, packing it ⅛- to ¼-inch thick. Cover with plastic wrap and refrigerate for 6 to 8 hours. (Do not cure the fish any longer than 8 hours or it will "overcook.")

Rinse the cure from the fish under gently running cold water, pat dry with a paper towel, cover with plastic wrap and refrigerate until needed or for up to 5 days. *Continued overleaf >*

Horseradish-mustard vinaigrette In a small bowl, whisk together mustards, red wine vinegar, horseradish, lemon juice and honey. Whisking constantly or using a handheld blender, gradually add sunflower (or canola) oil in a thin steady stream until fully incorporated and emulsified. Season with salt and pepper to taste. Set vinaigrette aside or transfer to an airtight container and refrigerate for up to 1 month. (Keep it only 2 to 3 days if you have added any fresh ingredients such as herbs, garlic or shallots.)

Warm potato salad In a small bowl, combine saffron and boiling water to make a "saffron tea." Cover with plastic wrap and set aside to steep for 10 minutes.

Wash and scrub potatoes, then cut in ⅜-inch-thick rounds. Place potatoes in a large pot and add enough water to just cover. Add saffron tea. Bring to a boil on high heat, then reduce the heat to low and simmer until potatoes are tender but resist slightly when pierced with a knife, 10 to 15 minutes.

Drain in a colander and allow to cool. Transfer to a medium bowl, drizzle lightly with olive oil and set aside.

Dijon dill mayonnaise In a small bowl, mix mayonnaise, dill and mustard until well combined.

Finish salmon and potato salad Preheat the oven to 300°F. Line a baking sheet with parchment paper.

Unwrap salmon and, using a sharp knife, cut the fillet on an angle into 12 slices, each about 1 inch thick. Arrange salmon pieces on the baking sheet, leaving 1 inch between them. Bake until just warm, 3 to 4 minutes. (The salmon should still be blue rare.)

In a large bowl, toss potatoes with 3 Tbsp of the horseradish-mustard vinaigrette, then transfer to the centre of a large serving platter. Top with salmon fillets, then drizzle 4 Tbsp of the Dijon dill mayonnaise over the fish in a zigzag pattern.

In a small bowl, lightly toss cilantro with lemon juice and garnish the dish. Lightly sprinkle with Maldon salt. Serve immediately, family-style.

Seared Salmon
with Shrimp Broth

1 lb raw shrimp, rinsed, peeled and deveined

½ cup dry white wine

1 cup fish stock (page 154)

Juice of ½ lemon (about 1 Tbsp)

Shrimp broth

1 Tbsp vegetable oil

½ cup roughly chopped onions

½ cup roughly chopped carrots

1 leek, white part only, well rinsed and cut in ½-inch slices (about ½ cup)

1 cup roughly chopped tomatoes

2 garlic cloves, crushed

½ tsp freshly grated ginger

one 1-inch piece of lemon grass, chopped

Seared salmon

4 wild spring or steelhead salmon fillets, each 4 oz, skin removed

2 Tbsp vegetable oil

2 Tbsp butter

2 Tbsp finely chopped shallots

1 bunch spinach, well washed and stems trimmed

1 Tbsp finely chopped fresh chives

THIS light and refreshing dish is a huge hit in our home. My kids just love salmon, but the broth is the real star in this recipe. Start with a good fish stock, which you can make from scratch in half an hour: just be sure your bones are very fresh and well rinsed before you begin. To make this broth a soup, add broccoli, cauliflower or asparagus and pieces of fresh cod or salmon. Serves 4

Shrimp broth Heat vegetable oil in a large pot on medium and add onions, carrots, leeks, tomatoes, garlic, ginger and lemon grass. Reduce the heat to medium-low and sauté, stirring occasionally, until vegetables are soft and glossy, 5 to 6 minutes. Add shrimp and cook, stirring, until bright pink, about 3 minutes. Deglaze the pan with white wine, then pour in fish stock and allow to simmer for 10 minutes. Strain broth through a fine-mesh sieve into a clean pot. Reserve the solids. Add lemon juice to the broth and season with salt and white pepper. Set aside, with the lid on.

Transfer shrimp from the sieve to an airtight container. Discard the remaining solids. Refrigerate shrimp for up to 1 day and use in a sandwich (page 36) instead of spot prawns or in crab cakes.

Seared salmon Preheat the oven to 375°F. Season salmon with salt and pepper.

Heat vegetable oil in an ovenproof frying pan on medium-high. Place salmon in pan and sear on one side until golden brown, 2 to 3 minutes. Turn salmon over, place the pan in the oven and cook for 3 to 4 minutes or until flesh is just opaque when poked at its thickest point with a knife. Remove from the oven, cover loosely with aluminum foil and set aside.

Heat a large frying pan on medium and add butter. While the butter is melting, add shallots and cook briefly, about 1 minute. Add spinach and, stirring constantly, toss it around the pan until wilted. Season with salt and pepper to taste. Keep warm until ready to serve.

To serve Divide the spinach among 4 warm bowls. Top with a piece of salmon and spoon 3 Tbsp of the shrimp broth around the fish. Sprinkle with a pinch of coarse salt and the chopped chives.

Cod **Tacos**

with My Salsa, Sweet and Sour Cabbage,
and Sambal Mayonnaise

6 oz cod, in 1-inch cubes

½ tsp Maldon salt

¼ tsp freshly ground black pepper

1 cup shredded green cabbage

1 Tbsp apple cider vinegar

½ tsp granulated sugar

1 cup cherry tomatoes
(about 12), sliced in half

1 Tbsp diced red onions

1 Tbsp chopped cilantro

1 tsp fresh lime juice

1 tsp finely chopped jalapeño peppers

1 ripe avocado, peeled,
pitted and roughly chopped

⅓ cup fresh corn kernels,
cooked 1 to 2 minutes

1 Tbsp extra-virgin olive oil

12 small flour tortillas, each 5 to 6 inches

⅓ cup sambal mayonnaise (page 159)

1 lime, in wedges

RICHARD JAFFRAY, the founder and president of Cactus Restaurants, has introduced me to surfing both in Tofino and Hawaii. When I'm looking for a simple but fun food to enjoy after a day on the waves, I can only think of one thing—a darn good taco. Fresh fish, salsa and some heat add up to just that. Grill the tortillas and fish on the barbecue for a real taste of summer.

As a substitute for cod, use prawns, halibut, rock fish, steelhead salmon, scallops or any fish that is fresh, local and sustainable. **Serves 4**

Season cod with ¼ tsp of the salt and a few grinds of black pepper and set aside.

Toss cabbage with apple cider vinegar and sugar in a small bowl and set aside.

In a bowl, combine tomatoes with onions, cilantro, lime juice, jalapeños, avocado and corn. Season with the remaining ¼ tsp salt and a few grinds of black pepper, and toss gently to avoid mashing the avocado. Season with more salt, if needed. Set salsa aside.

Preheat a stovetop grill or a barbecue to high. In a frying pan, heat olive oil on medium-high. When oil is hot, add cod and sear, lightly tossing fish, until all sides of the cubes are cooked, 2 to 3 minutes. Using a slotted spoon, transfer cod to a warm plate, loosely cover with aluminum foil and set in a warm place.

In the meantime, grill tortillas for 10 seconds per side. (Or warm them in a nonstick pan on medium-high for 20 seconds per side.)

To assemble, place tortillas on a clean work surface. Spoon 2 Tbsp of the fish onto each tortilla, then add 2 Tbsp cabbage and a dash of salsa and top with a spoonful of spicy mayonnaise. Fold the bottom of each tortilla over the filling, then fold one side over the other to encase the filling. Serve at once with lime wedges on the side.

Pan-Fried **Wild Snapper**

with Israeli Couscous Ragout

Couscous ragout

2 cups roasted tomato sauce (page 161)

2 Tbsp capers, rinsed

2 Tbsp currants

1 cup cooked Israeli couscous

½ cup chopped grilled
red bell peppers (page 7)

2 Tbsp chopped Kalamata olives

2 Tbsp pine nuts

1 tsp salt

¼ tsp black pepper

2 Tbsp chopped mixed fresh rosemary,
thyme and parsley

Israeli couscous

½ cup dry Israeli couscous

1 Tbsp unsalted butter

2 Tbsp diced onions

1 cup chicken stock (page 155)

½ tsp salt

⅛ tsp black pepper

WHEN you can get wild red snapper, this is a fun and simple way to prepare it. If it's not available, use another firm-textured fish, such as lingcod. The currants, the combination of herbs and the olives in the ragout give this dish a very southern French and Spanish flavour.

Charlie Trotter introduced me to Israeli couscous years ago, and though it took me a while to find it then, it is now widely available. Larger than the small, fluffy Moroccan couscous grains I was used to, Israeli couscous has a pasta-like texture that is delicious on its own or served with poultry or fish dishes in a sauce. Serve this ragout with poached chicken (page 108), steamed greens or salad greens or use it as a filling for zucchini, summer squash or bell peppers. **Serves 4**

Israeli couscous Preheat the oven to 250°F. Place couscous in a small oven-proof pan and toast in the oven until lightly brown, 5 to 8 minutes. Remove from the oven and set aside.

Heat a small pot on medium-high. Add butter and onions and sauté for 2 to 3 minutes, until translucent. Stir in couscous, chicken stock, salt and pepper. Bring to a boil, then reduce the heat to low. Cover and simmer, stirring frequently, for 15 minutes. If the pot is dry and the couscous is still crunchy, add 1 to 2 Tbsp chicken stock (or water) and cook for another 5 minutes, or until just tender. Drain off any remaining liquid and fluff with a fork.

Red Snapper

1 Tbsp vegetable oil	1 sprig fresh thyme
4 fillets red snapper, each 6 oz, skin on	Rind of ½ lemon, coarsely grated
½ tsp salt	1 Tbsp extra-virgin olive oil
2 Tbsp cold butter	Pinch of Maldon salt

Couscous ragout In a medium pot on medium heat, combine tomato sauce, capers, currants, couscous, grilled peppers, olives and pine nuts and slowly bring to a boil. Season with salt, pepper and mixed herbs. Reduce the heat to low and simmer gently until heated through and flavours are combined, about 5 minutes. Set aside, or allow to cool and refrigerate in an airtight container for up to 3 days.

Red snapper Heat a large frying pan on medium-high and add vegetable oil. Season both sides of snapper with the ½ tsp of salt. When the oil is hot, place fillets, skin side down, in the pan. (If you prefer skinless fish, either cook the fish with the skin on and remove it after or cook the best-looking side of the skinless fillets first.) Sear for 2 minutes, or until golden, then turn fish over, flipping it away from you to avoid splattering the oil. Cook for 1 minute. Add butter, thyme and lemon rind and cook for 1 minute more. Using a spoon, baste snapper constantly with hot pan juices to finish cooking the fish. It is ready when the flesh resists slightly when touched lightly with your fingertip. (The total cooking time for a snapper fillet that is 1 inch thick is 7 to 8 minutes.)

To serve Place the ragout in a large serving bowl and top with the red snapper fillets. Garnish with a drizzle of olive oil and a pinch of Maldon salt. Serve immediately.

Grilled **Scallops**

with Corn, Bacon and Red Pepper Ragout

1 Tbsp soy sauce

1 Tbsp rice vinegar

1 Tbsp fresh lemon juice

2 slices smoked bacon, in ¼-inch dice

½ cup diced red onions

1 cup corn kernels, cut off the cob

½ red bell pepper, in ¼-inch dice (about ½ cup)

1 Thai chili, seeded and finely minced

Juice of 1 lime (about 1 Tbsp)

1 Tbsp unsalted butter

12 large scallops (muscles removed from sides, if present)

1 tsp extra-virgin olive oil

1 Tbsp finely chopped cilantro

THIS dish makes an excellent starter for a meal or a nice lunch when served with a simple green salad. I use Qualicum Bay scallops and peaches-and-cream corn, both of which are local products, but you can substitute other varieties of either. The hot and salty ragout is an especially good combination with scallops, but it's also delicious with baked halibut or grilled steelhead salmon. Serves 4

In a small bowl, combine soy sauce, rice vinegar and lemon juice. Set aside.

Heat a large frying pan on medium. Add the bacon and cook for 2 to 3 minutes, stirring, until crisp. Stir in onions, corn, bell peppers and chili and sauté for 2 minutes, then add lime juice and butter. Season with salt and pepper, reduce the heat to low and simmer while scallops are cooking. (Or refrigerate the ragout in an airtight container for up to 2 days.)

Preheat a stovetop grill or a barbecue to medium-high. Warm a plate in the oven at 200°F. Pat scallops dry with paper towels and season with salt, pepper and a dash of olive oil. Grill scallops for 2 minutes, turn over and grill for another 1 minute. Transfer to the warm plate.

Divide the ragout evenly among 4 plates and top each serving with 3 scallops. Spoon about 2 tsp of the soy dressing over each plate and garnish with cilantro. Serve immediately.

Grilled **Spot Prawns**

with Chili, Soy and Lime

1 tsp sesame seeds

2 tsp granulated sugar

2 Tbsp extra-virgin olive oil

4 Tbsp light soy sauce

1 Tbsp sesame oil

24 whole prawns

1 clove garlic, minced

2 tsp chili flakes

Juice of 1 lemon (about 2 Tbsp)

THIS is a very simple prawn recipe that tastes so darn good you'll want to make it often. Spot prawns are a sweet and delicate seafood that goes well with salty and spicy flavours. Here, it's the chili flakes that provide a little heat. They are an essential flavour for the dish but you can dial them back if you're not fond of spicy. **Serves 4**

In a small bowl, combine soy sauce, sesame oil, garlic, sesame seeds and sugar. Season to taste with freshly ground black pepper. Set aside.

In a large frying pan, heat olive oil on medium-high. Add prawns and sauté for 2 minutes. Add the soy-sesame mixture, chili flakes and lemon juice and cook for 1 to 2 minutes until liquid has reduced and coats the prawns. Serve immediately.

Mussels with Chorizo
and Spicy Tomato Sauce

1 Tbsp extra-virgin olive oil

8 oz smoked chorizo sausages,
in ¼-inch angled slices

¼ onion, in ¼-inch dice (about ¼ cup)

2 tsp minced garlic

2 tsp chili flakes

1 cup dry white wine

4 lbs mussels, scrubbed
clean and beards removed

2 cups (almost double the recipe)
tomato and basil sauce (page 161)

¼ cup chopped fresh flat-leaf parsley

THE VERY first time I really had a good bowl of mussels was in Belgium, the kingdom of mussels and fries. This version is based on the memory of that dish: fresh mussels, wine and chili flakes, with the big bonus of chorizo. Serve these mussels in warm bowls with a nice big loaf of crusty bread to soak up the juices.

Mussels need cleaning before you cook them. Although farmed mussels are generally cleaner to start with than wild ones, place all mussels in a large bowl and let them sit under a tap of slowly running cold water for half an hour. Inspect the mussels and, if necessary, brush off any dirt still clinging to the shells and pull off any beards with a small paring knife or needle-nose pliers. Discard any mussels with broken shells or open shells that don't close when tapped. Rinse the mussels thoroughly before you begin. Serves 4

Heat a large pot on medium and add olive oil. Add chorizo and sauté for 2 minutes. When chorizo begins to brown and curl, add onions and sauté until soft, about 5 minutes. Stir in garlic and chili flakes, cook for another 2 minutes and then deglaze the pan with white wine, stirring loose the caramelized bits from the bottom of the pan.

Add mussels, cover and cook for 2 to 3 minutes. Stir in tomato sauce and continue cooking until the mussels have opened and sauce has reduced slightly, about 5 minutes. Discard any mussels that do not open. Stir in parsley. Season with salt and pepper, if necessary. Divide into 4 warm bowls and serve immediately.

POULTRY & MEATS

Poached **Chicken**

1 whole free-range chicken, 2 to 3 lbs

16 cups cold water

2 cups roughly chopped white onions

2 cups roughly chopped celery

2 cups roughly chopped carrots

1 bunch fresh thyme

1 Tbsp whole white peppercorns

4 bay leaves

As a young chef studying in Burgundy, I had a dish made from a poached chicken breast that is still among the best meals I've ever eaten. And this is one of the first recipes I learned. It is incredibly versatile because it produces not only succulent chicken but an incredible chicken stock. From this one poached chicken, you can create chicken soup (page 35), chicken pot pie (page 109) and spaghetti with chicken and chanterelles (page 77), to name just a few possibilities. Serves 4

CHEF'S TIP When working with raw chicken, be sure to scrub with hot soapy water all surfaces and utensils that come into contact with the chicken, including your hands.

Using a small, sharp knife, remove and discard all the skin from the chicken. Rinse chicken well under cold running water. Place chicken in a very large deep pot and add the 16 cups of cold water, onions, celery, carrots, thyme, peppercorns and bay leaves. Bring to a boil on high heat, then reduce the heat to low and allow the mixture to simmer, covered, for 30 minutes. Using a slotted spoon, skim as much fat off the surface as you can.

Transfer chicken from the stock to a shallow pan (using long tongs inserted into the cavity or a large sieve to lift it out of the stock) and allow to cool. While chicken is cooling, line a fine-mesh sieve with cheesecloth, strain stock and set aside. Discard the solids. This light-tasting broth is good as a soup base and will keep refrigerated in an airtight container for 3 to 4 days.

Using your hands, pull the chicken meat off the bones and discard the carcass. Allow to cool completely, then transfer to an airtight container and refrigerate for up to 3 days. The chicken will also keep frozen, tightly wrapped in plastic wrap and double bagged, for up to 1 month.

Chicken **Pot Pie**

¼ cup vegetable oil

½ cup diced onions

½ cup diced carrots

½ cup diced celery

½ cup diced parsnips

½ cup diced leeks, white part only

3 cups chicken stock (page 155)

1 poached chicken (page 108),
cooked meat shredded

1 Tbsp salt

1 tsp black pepper

2 Tbsp unsalted butter, softened

2 Tbsp all-purpose flour

½ cup whipping cream

½ cup fresh or frozen green peas

½ recipe pâte brisée (page 163)

1 egg beaten with 1 Tbsp water (egg wash)

THIS recipe is the reason I wanted to become a chef. My mother used to make the best chicken pot pie on the planet, and this dish is now not only dear to my heart but also comforting to the soul. For best results, cut all the vegetables in half-inch dice. If you want to kick up this basic recipe, which I've adapted from the one Mom made for us as kids, add either half a cup of fresh morel mushrooms or two tablespoons of dried ones. Turn it into a vegetable pot pie by increasing the number of veggies and using vegetable stock. Serves 6

Have six 1-cup ovenproof bowls or a 6- to 8-cup ovenproof casserole dish at the ready. Heat a medium stockpot on medium-high. Add vegetable oil and, when hot, add onions and cook for 4 to 5 minutes, until translucent. Stir in carrots, celery, parsnips and leeks and cook for another 2 to 3 minutes. Pour in chicken stock and cook for 10 minutes, stirring occasionally.

Add shredded chicken and season with salt and pepper. In a small bowl, combine butter and flour until well mixed. Add this roux paste to the pot and whisk constantly until free of lumps. Add whipping cream, reduce the heat to medium-low and simmer for 2 to 3 minutes until flour is completely cooked and the gravy has thickened a little and coats the back of a spoon. Stir in peas. Season with salt, if necessary. Divide the mixture evenly among the 6 ovenproof bowls (or transfer it to a large casserole dish).

Preheat the oven to 425°F.

On a clean work surface, use a rolling pin to roll out the pastry ⅛-inch thick. Using a sharp knife, cut six rounds, each 1 inch larger than the diameter of the ovenproof bowls (or one sheet slightly larger than the casserole dish). Place a pastry round on top of each bowl (or place the pastry onto the casserole dish) and press it firmly onto the edge of the bowls. Brush the top of the pastry with the egg wash. Cut vents in the top of each pie to allow steam to escape. Bake until the pastry is golden brown and juices are bubbling, about 15 minutes.

Poached **Chicken**

with Morel and Asparagus Cream

1 lb white asparagus, trimmed and peeled

1 lb green asparagus, trimmed and peeled

6 to 8 cups chicken stock (page 155)

1 whole free-range chicken, 3 to 4 lbs

1 Tbsp unsalted butter

1 shallot, thinly sliced

2 cups morel (or crimini) mushrooms, cleaned

¼ cup dry white wine

1 cup whipping cream

freshly ground white pepper

THIS delicious dish is made with local British Columbia produce but inspired by the chicken in morel mushroom cream I ate in a small two-star Michelin restaurant in Burgundy many years ago. Open a nice bottle of Macon-Villages or a good red burgundy to go with it, or sip a good B.C. Pinot Noir. Serves 4

Fill a large bowl with ice water. Bring a large pot of salted water to a boil on high heat. Add white and green asparagus to the boiling water, reduce the heat to medium and simmer, uncovered, for 4 minutes. Remove the pot from the heat and set aside for 3 to 4 minutes, still uncovered, until spears are just tender. Drain asparagus in a colander and immediately plunge it into the ice water. When cool, drain asparagus again and set aside.

In a pot just large enough to hold the whole chicken and the liquid, bring chicken stock to a boil on medium heat. (If you are using the basic chicken stock recipe from this book, which contains no salt, add ½ tsp salt. Do not add salt if you are using commercial stock, which often contains salt.) Carefully lower the chicken into the stock and poach at a gentle simmer for 30 to 35 minutes, or until the temperature of the innermost part of the thigh is 180°F. Remove chicken from stock by inserting long tongs into the cavity to lift it (hold a dry, folded kitchen towel in your other hand to support the wet fowl as well) and place on a platter. Cover loosely with aluminum foil.

Reheat 4 cups of the chicken stock on medium-high and reduce by half, 15 to 20 minutes. (The rest of the stock can be strained, cooled and refrigerated or frozen for another use.)

Melt butter in a medium saucepan on medium heat, add shallots and cook for 2 minutes. Cut any very large mushrooms in half, then add all of them to the saucepan. Cook for 2 to 3 minutes, then add white wine and reduce by half, about 5 minutes. Add reduced stock and again reduce by half, about 10 minutes. Add whipping cream and reduce by one-third, about 10 minutes. Season to taste with salt and freshly ground white pepper. Cut asparagus into 1-inch pieces and add to the shallot-mushroom sauce.

Carve chicken into 8 pieces: 2 drumsticks, 2 thighs and 4 breast pieces with wings (cutting each side of the breast in half). Place 4 pieces of chicken in the centre of a large platter and top with half of the asparagus-mushroom sauce. Repeat the layering with the remaining 4 pieces of chicken and the remaining asparagus-mushroom sauce. This dish will keep refrigerated in an airtight container for up to 2 days.

Cornish **Game Hen**

with Dried Fruit, Honey and Almonds

3 Tbsp extra-virgin olive oil

½ cup blanched whole almonds

1 cup dried fruits (any one of,
or a mixture of, dates, apricots, prunes)

2 Cornish game hens, about 1½ lbs each

2 medium onions, in ¼-inch dice

2 cups water

½ cup finely chopped
fresh flat-leaf parsley

2 Tbsp minced fresh ginger

1 tsp ground cinnamon

½ tsp ground nutmeg

Pinch of ground cloves

¼ cup honey

⅓ cup raisins

From 2000 to 2004, I did a television show on Food Network Canada called *New Classics with Chef Rob Feenie*. For the show, I developed this recipe, which was inspired by a trip to Egypt as a teenager, and I still make it often for company. It uses a local bird but adds a Middle Eastern twist—the fruits, spices and nuts—that is highly addictive. It's a light but flavourful dish that's great served with a side of steamed rice or couscous salad. Dress it up with a garnish of fresh mint or chervil, pistachios, preserved lemon slices and/or dollops of cumin-spiked Greek yogurt. Serves 4 to 6

Line a large plate with paper towels. Heat 1 Tbsp of the olive oil in a large frying pan on medium. Add almonds and sauté until golden, 7 to 8 minutes. Using a slotted spoon, transfer to the plate to drain. Set aside.

Prepare dried fruits by pitting dates (discard the pits) and cutting large apricots and prunes in half. Set aside.

Cut game hens into quarters (2 breasts and 2 legs per bird). With a paper towel, pat game hens dry and season with salt and black pepper. Heat the remaining 2 Tbsp of oil in a large frying pan on medium-high heat. Arrange hen pieces in the pan and sauté until golden brown on all sides, about 5 minutes. Using a slotted spoon, transfer hen pieces to a plate and set aside.

Add onions to the pan and sauté until translucent and softened, about 10 minutes, stirring up the brown bits from the bottom of the pan. Return the hen pieces to the pan and add the 2 cups of water, parsley, ginger, cinnamon, nutmeg and cloves. Bring to a boil, then reduce the heat to low and simmer, covered, for about 35 minutes or until cooked. To test for doneness, insert a sharp knife in a thigh piece. If the juices run clear yellow with no tinge of red, the hen pieces are cooked. Transfer hen pieces to a large plate and cover loosely with aluminum foil.

Increase the heat to medium. Add dried fruits, honey and raisins to the pan and simmer until fruits are soft and the juices have reduced and thickened somewhat, about 15 minutes. Return hen pieces to the pan and reheat quickly, basting with the juices. Transfer the game hen pieces and fruit mixture to a large serving platter, sprinkle with almonds and serve immediately. This dish will keep refrigerated in an airtight container for up to 2 days.

Grilled Quail *on Eggplant and Goat Cheese "Lasagna"*

with Herbed Game Jus

Grilled quail

1 Tbsp + 4 tsp extra-virgin olive oil

¼ tsp minced garlic

¼ tsp chopped fresh rosemary

8 partially boned quail,
leg and wing bones left in

Eggplant and goat cheese "lasagna"

3 Tbsp + 2 tsp salt

2 large eggplants, peeled and cut
crosswise in ½-inch disks (at least 12)

3 Tbsp + 4 tsp extra-virgin olive oil

½ tsp black pepper

1 cup soft goat cheese

6 Tbsp panko crumbs

1 cup tomato and basil sauce (page 161)

1 Tbsp fresh basil in chiffonade

¼ cup freshly grated Parmesan cheese

Herbed game jus

½ cup port wine

1 cup dark chicken stock (page 155)

2 Tbsp peeled, seeded
and chopped tomatoes

1 Tbsp chopped fresh flat-leaf parsley

½ tsp chopped fresh basil

½ tsp chopped fresh thyme

2 Tbsp unsalted butter, cold

¼ tsp freshly ground black pepper

Fava-shallot sauté

2 Tbsp unsalted butter

2 Tbsp chopped shallots

2 cups shelled fava beans (or lima beans)

1 tsp salt

½ tsp freshly group pepper

1 lemon

4 sprigs fresh thyme

PARTIALLY boned quail (called "boneless" quail in markets) are easier to use and much easier to eat than the whole bird. Ask your butcher to bring them in for you. Serve this layered "lasagna" on warm plates as a main course or a side dish with lamb or roast chicken. Serves 4

Grilled quail In a large bowl, mix 1 Tbsp of the olive oil with garlic and rosemary. Add quail and coat well with marinade. Cover the bowl (or transfer quail and marinade to a resealable plastic bag) and refrigerate for at least 2 hours.

Eggplant and goat cheese "lasagna" Lightly oil four 1-cup ovenproof soufflé dishes and line the bottom of each with a circle of parchment paper. Line a baking sheet with parchment paper.

Fill a large bowl with cold water and stir in the 3 Tbsp salt. Add eggplant slices, placing a plate on them to keep them submerged, and soak for about 20 minutes. Drain eggplant in a colander and pat dry with paper towels.

Preheat the oven to 350°F. Using a pastry brush, brush eggplant on both sides with olive oil and season lightly with the 2 tsp salt and the pepper. Arrange eggplant on the baking sheet and bake for 10 minutes. Turn eggplant slices over and roast for another 10 minutes, or until soft and lightly browned. Set aside.

Divide goat cheese into 8 portions. Roll each piece of cheese into a ball, then flatten into discs about 3 inches in diameter (or similar in diameter to the eggplant). Set aside.

Choose 12 slices of eggplant of similar size. Find the 4 most attractive pieces and place 1 of them in the bottom of each soufflé dish (trim eggplant if it is too large). Sprinkle each slice with 2 tsp of panko crumbs and place a goat cheese round on top. Spoon 2 Tbsp of tomato sauce into each dish, add a pinch of basil and top with 1½ tsp of Parmesan cheese. Top with another slice of eggplant and repeat the layering, ending with an eggplant slice. You should have 3 layers of eggplant and 2 layers of filling. Gently press everything down with your fingers.

Place soufflé dishes on the baking sheet and bake for 20 to 25 minutes. Remove from the oven and set aside.

Finish quail Remove quail from the refrigerator and allow to stand at room temperature for about 10 minutes. Heat 2 large frying pans on medium-high and add 2 tsp of olive oil to each. Place quail in the pans, breast side down, and sear until golden brown with crispy skin, 4 to 5 minutes. Turn quail over and cook for another 2 to 3 minutes, or until the meat resists when pressed lightly. (Quail breast is most tender when cooked to medium or medium rare.) Transfer cooked quail to a platter and allow to rest in a warm place for 5 to 7 minutes.

Herbed game jus Discard any burned pieces of garlic or rosemary from the frying pan in which you cooked the quail. Add port wine and, using a wooden spoon, scrape the caramelized bits from the bottom of the pan to deglaze it.

In a small bowl, combine chicken stock, tomatoes, parsley, basil and thyme. Add this mixture to the frying pan and cook on medium-low heat for 10 minutes, or until liquid is reduced by half. Add butter and swirl in the pan until incorporated and until the sauce has thickened slightly and is shiny, 2 to 3 minutes. Season with black pepper and salt to taste. Set aside.

Fava-shallot sauté Heat a small frying pan on medium and add butter. Stir in shallots and cook for 1 minute, or until soft. Add fava beans and cook for another 2 minutes. Season with salt, pepper and lemon juice.

To serve Place a warm plate over each soufflé dish. Carefully invert the eggplant "lasagnas" to unmould them. Remove the parchment circles. Lean 2 quail against each eggplant lasagna and spoon a quarter of the fava beans on top. Spoon herbed jus evenly over each serving and garnish with a sprig of fresh thyme. Leftover quail can be refrigerated in an airtight container for up to 1 day.

Gascon-Style **Duck Stew**

with Olives and Fennel Seeds

1 whole duck

1 tsp salt

1 tsp black pepper

4 Tbsp extra-virgin olive oil

8 oz pancetta, in ¼-inch dice

1 onion, in ¼-inch dice (about 1 cup)

3 ribs celery, in ¼-inch dice (about 1 cup)

2 small carrots, in ¼-inch dice (about 1 cup)

1 Tbsp fennel seeds

1½ cups green Lucques olives

1 cup sweet red vermouth

3 cups (double the recipe) tomato and basil sauce (page 161)

1 tsp chili flakes

THIS classic dish reminds me of southern France, duck confit and cassoulet. It's a great way to experience local duck, using the fat wisely and in a way that will make you fall in love with both duck fat and this dish. Although I am not as huge a fan of olives as my kids and my wife are, they are magical with the duck. And, like many dishes in this book, the flavour of this stew gets better and better with reheating. If you have leftovers, the stew makes a great sauce for pasta.

If you prefer not to do the job yourself, the butcher will cut up the duck for you. You want ten pieces. Ask for all the excess fat, fatty skin, meaty scraps and any bones. The fat and fatty skin can be rendered in a pot on low heat, then refrigerated in an airtight glass container to make duck confit or to fry potatoes. The meaty scraps make a tasty stock. All scraps and rendered fat freeze well.

This dish is a perfect fit with the quinoa, green bean and tomato salad (page 53), and is also excellent with soft polenta (page 61) or pasta. Serves 6 to 8

Using a sharp knife, split duck in half along its backbone. Remove both legs at the joints that attach them to backbone. Separate the drumsticks from the thighs. Remove the wings by cutting through the joints that attach them to the breast. You may remove the wing tips and freeze them with the meaty scraps. Cut each side of the breast in half. (You should have 10 pieces: 2 drumsticks, 2 thighs, 2 wings and 4 breast pieces.) Trim and tidy up these pieces. With a paper towel, pat duck pieces dry and season with salt and pepper.

In a large heavy-bottomed braising pan or a Dutch oven, heat olive oil on medium-high until it smokes. Working in batches, if necessary, place duck, skin side down, in the hot pan and cook until golden brown and most of the fat has been rendered, 5 to 8 minutes. Transfer duck pieces to a plate and set aside.

Drain all but 2 Tbsp of fat from the pan. Reduce the heat to medium, add pancetta and cook until lightly browned, about 5 minutes. Stir in onions, celery, carrots and fennel seeds and cook until vegetables are softened, about 10 minutes. Add olives, vermouth, tomato sauce and chili flakes and bring to a boil. Add duck, submerging each piece in the liquid. Reduce the heat to low. Cover and simmer for 1½ hours, or until duck is tender and falling off the bone.

Transfer duck stew to a large bowl and serve.

Meatballs *with Dipping Sauce*

Basic meatball dipping sauce

2 cups roasted tomato sauce (page 161)

1 cup balsamic reduction (page 159)

Spicy meatball dipping sauce

2 cups roasted tomato sauce (page 161)

1 cup spicy barbecue sauce (page 160)

Meatballs

½ baguette, crusts removed,
roughly torn (4 cups large pieces)

½ cup whole milk

½ cup water

1½ lbs lean ground beef chuck

1 lb ground pork

4 eggs, beaten

1 cup finely minced onions

1 Tbsp chopped garlic

¼ cup chopped fresh flat-leaf parsley

1 Tbsp chopped fresh thyme

2 tsp salt

1 tsp freshly ground black pepper

½ cup freshly grated Parmesan cheese

½ cup all-purpose flour (optional)

½ cup vegetable oil, for pan-frying

MY MOTHER-IN-LAW, Trish, will argue that her meatballs are the best. And, you know, she may be right, as my kids and my wife love them. This recipe is for all of them. It makes a great snack or an appetizer with dipping sauces or a cucumber and yogurt dip, or use it to turn basic pasta into a plate of spaghetti and meatballs. In a sandwich, combine sliced meatballs with bocconcini cheese, tomato and arugula. Lightly coating the meatballs in flour before cooking them creates a crust that adds another dimension to their texture.

Each of these dipping sauces makes about 3 cups. Make just one version, or serve them both in separate bowls. Refrigerate any leftovers in an airtight container for up to three days or freeze them for up to a month. **Makes about 40 meatballs**

CHEF'S TIP If mixing meatballs by hand, use disposable gloves for a tidier process.

Meatball dipping sauces For each sauce: Use a food processor or hand-held blender to purée tomato sauce. Transfer to a small pot and set on medium heat. Add balsamic reduction (or barbecue sauce) and heat for 5 minutes. Spoon into a warm bowl or sauce boat and serve.

Meatballs Place bread, milk and water in a medium bowl. Allow bread to soak for about 5 minutes, then carefully transfer to a colander. Discard the soaking liquid, and squeeze out and discard excess liquid from the bread.

Place bread in the bowl of a stand mixer with a paddle attachment (or in a large bowl). Add beef, pork, eggs, onions, garlic, parsley, thyme, salt, pepper and Parmesan cheese and mix thoroughly. Using your hands or a small spoon, form the mixture into balls about 1½ inches in diameter. (You should have about 40.)

Preheat the oven to 375°F. Place the flour on a large plate, if using.

Heat a heavy-bottomed frying pan on medium-high and add vegetable oil. Roll the meatballs, a few at a time, in the flour, shaking off any excess. Carefully place them into the hot oil. (Cook meatballs in batches so as not to crowd the pan.) Cook, shaking the pan or moving the meatballs around with a spoon to brown them evenly, keep their round shape and prevent them from sticking, for about 5 minutes per batch. Transfer cooked meatballs to a baking sheet. Bake meatballs for 10 minutes, or until a meat thermometer inserted in the middle reads 160°F. Cooked meatballs will keep refrigerated in an airtight container for up to 3 days or frozen for up to 1 month.

Steak **Pot Pie**

1½ tsp salt

½ tsp black pepper

1¼ lbs top sirloin beef, in 1-inch cubes, patted dry with paper towels

4 Tbsp vegetable oil

½ onion, in ¼-inch dice (about ½ cup)

1 cup Guinness beer

1 cup veal stock (page 156)

10 pearl onions, unpeeled

1 large parsnip, in 1-inch pieces (about ½ cup)

1 clip top turnip, in ½-inch pieces (about ½ cup)

1 large carrot, in 1-inch pieces (about ½ cup)

WHEN I was a kid, my mom would make these pies at least once a month, and I loved them. As usual, I have added a few of my own secret ingredients, including some veal stock and some Guinness. (This filling also works well as a stew with side dishes or as a base for shepherd's pie.)

To save time, you can prepare the pastry ahead of time, and even roll it and cut it into pieces. Cover each piece with a square of waxed paper, stack them and tightly wrap the entire stack in plastic wrap. Refrigerate the pastry for up to two days. Allow the pastry to soften at room temperature for fifteen minutes before filling and cooking it. Serves 4

Combine salt and pepper in a small bowl, then season beef with half of the mixture.

Heat a large sauté pan with a lid on medium-high. Add 2 Tbsp of the vegetable oil, then stir in beef, shaking the pan so the meat browns and cooks evenly on all sides, about 5 minutes total. Stir in diced onions and sauté for 5 minutes, or until onions are translucent and softened. Deglaze the pan with Guinness. Add veal stock and bring to a boil. Reduce the heat to low, until the mixture bubbles gently. Cover and simmer beef for 1 hour, or until tender.

While beef is cooking, prepare vegetables. Preheat the oven to 375°F. Have four 1-cup ovenproof bowls or ramekins ready.

Bring a small pot of water to a boil on high heat. Add pearl onions and blanch for about 20 seconds. Drain in a colander and set aside to cool slightly. Using your fingers or a small knife, peel off and discard the skins.

1 rib celery, in 1-inch pieces
(about ⅓ cup)

1 medium Yukon Gold potato,
in 1-inch dice (about 1 cup)

1 Tbsp chopped fresh thyme

1½ tsp butter, softened

1½ tsp all-purpose flour

2 Tbsp grainy mustard

½ cup whipping cream

½ recipe pâte brisée (page 163)

1 egg, beaten with
1 Tbsp water (egg wash)

In a roasting pan, combine pearl onions, parsnips, turnips, carrots, celery, and potatoes. Toss with the remaining 2 Tbsp of vegetable oil and the remaining salt and pepper. Sprinkle with thyme and roast in the oven for 15 minutes or until tender, stirring occasionally. Remove from the oven and set aside. Increase the oven temperature to 425°F (or 400°F, if using a convection oven).

In a small bowl, combine butter and flour and knead to form a soft roux paste. Set aside. When the beef is done, add the roasted vegetables to the sauté pan, stir in mustard and cook for another 5 minutes. Then add the roux paste a little at a time, whisking constantly to prevent lumps, incorporate it evenly and thicken the filling. Pour in whipping cream and simmer the beef mixture for 2 to 3 minutes more, until flour is completely cooked. Divide the beef mixture among the 4 bowls (or ramekins).

On a clean, lightly floured work surface, use a rolling pin to roll out the pastry ⅛-inch thick. Using a sharp knife, cut 4 rounds, each 1 inch larger than the oven-proof bowls. Place a pastry round on top of each bowl and press firmly onto the edges. Brush the top of the pastry with the egg wash. Cut vents in the top of each pie to allow steam to escape. Bake until the pastry is golden brown and juices are bubbling, about 15 minutes. Serve immediately.

Braised **Beef Short Ribs**

3 lbs boneless beef short ribs

2 tsp salt

½ tsp black pepper

2 Tbsp extra-virgin olive oil

½ cup roughly chopped celery

½ cup roughly chopped carrots

½ cup roughly chopped onions

2 cups dry red wine

4 cups chicken stock (page 155)

2 to 4 cups veal stock (page 156)

2 sprigs fresh thyme

4 sprigs fresh rosemary

Handful of fresh parsley stems

1 Tbsp whole black peppercorns

½ cup roughly chopped fresh tomatoes

4 cloves garlic, peeled but left whole

I SIMPLY love to make short ribs on a regular basis. Braising is a good way to use less-expensive cuts of meat. (Because of their recent popularity short ribs have gone up in price, but spending the extra money is still well worth it.) Braising is also a good way to prepare dishes ahead of time: these short ribs can be reheated quickly, and a resting period allows their flavours to meld.

Serve this dish as an entrée or use the meat for pastas, warm beef-dip sandwiches or a very good steak and kidney pie. The leftover braising liquid is a great base sauce for any meat dish and even for fish and poultry. This is one of my favourite dishes—enjoy. Serves 4 to 6

Preheat the oven to 275°F. With a paper towel, pat short ribs dry and season all sides with the salt and pepper.

Heat a large frying pan on medium and add olive oil. When the oil is hot, carefully add short ribs, in batches if necessary, being careful not to splatter oil. Sear meat on all sides until dark golden brown, 2 to 3 minutes per side. Transfer to a deep-sided ceramic or stainless steel roasting pan.

Add celery, carrots and onions to the frying pan and sauté until caramelized and deep brown, about 10 minutes. Deglaze the pan with red wine, scraping up the brown bits on the bottom of the pan. Cook for 30 seconds, then slowly add chicken stock and 2 cups of the veal stock. Add thyme, rosemary, parsley, peppercorns, tomatoes and garlic, and bring to a boil. Pour the hot liquid over the short ribs, adding more veal stock, if necessary, to just cover the meat. Cover with a lid or aluminum foil, and cook in the oven for 3½ hours, or until short ribs are fork tender.

Fill a large roasting pan with ice water and set aside. Using a slotted spoon, carefully remove short ribs from the braising liquid and place them in a bowl. If serving the ribs as an entrée, cut into desired individual portions, about 6 oz, and serve immediately. If using in sandwiches or pasta, break up the meat into smaller pieces while it is still warm. (To reserve, set the bowl of meat in the ice water, stirring occasionally, to cool quickly, then refrigerate beef, wrapped in plastic in an airtight container, for up to 2 days.)

Strain the braising liquid through a fine-mesh sieve into a clean pot. Discard the solids. Bring the braising liquid to a boil on high heat, then reduce the heat to medium and reduce the liquid by half, about 10 minutes. Serve the braising liquid immediately over short ribs, or allow to cool and refrigerate it in an airtight container for up to 3 days or freeze for up to 1 month.

Riviera-Herbed **Leg of Lamb**

with Roasted Shallots and Sautéed Spinach

1 boneless leg of lamb,
4 lbs, butterflied

1 tsp sea salt

½ tsp black pepper

4 Tbsp extra-virgin olive oil

1 Tbsp cumin

2 Tbsp Dijon mustard

6 cloves garlic, finely chopped,
+ 2 cloves, peeled but left whole

2 Tbsp finely chopped
fresh flat-leaf parsley

2 Tbsp finely chopped fresh thyme

2 Tbsp finely chopped fresh rosemary

12 shallots, peeled

2 bunches spinach, washed
and large stems removed

3 Tbsp dry white wine

LAMB from New Zealand and Australia is readily available, usually frozen but occasionally fresh. If you can, however, search out local lamb from Vancouver Island or the Fraser Valley, both of which are very special and worth the extra price.

Prepare a variation that adds to the rub on this lamb by heating an oven-proof roasting pan on medium-high. Add a tablespoon of olive oil and brown the trussed lamb on all sides. Add one cup each of dry red wine and port wine, scrape up any brown bits on the bottom of the pan, cover and braise the lamb as directed in the recipe. If the liquid reduces too much while the lamb is cooking, add a quarter cup of water to prevent the sauce from becoming sticky. Serves 6 to 8

Season both sides of the lamb with salt and pepper. In a large bowl, combine 3 Tbsp of the olive oil, cumin, mustard, the finely chopped garlic, parsley, thyme and rosemary until well mixed. Rub lamb well all over with the rub, then place in a large ceramic or stainless steel pan, cover and refrigerate for at least 2 hours.

Preheat the oven to 325°F. Cut 7 pieces of kitchen string, each 12 inches. Place lamb on a clean work surface with the long side parallel to the edge. Pressing firmly with your hands, tightly roll the meat away from you to make a log and tie with kitchen string every 1½ inches so it keeps its shape while cooking. Place trussed lamb in a roasting pan with a lid (or cover with aluminum foil) and cook for 2¼ hours, basting occasionally with roasting juices. Add shallots to the pan and cook for 15 minutes more. Increase the heat to 425°F, remove the lid

(or foil) and roast for about 10 minutes until shallots are caramelized. Remove lamb from the oven, remove and discard the kitchen string and allow meat to rest for 10 minutes.

While lamb is resting, place the remaining 1 Tbsp of olive oil in a frying pan large enough to hold all of the cleaned spinach. Turn the heat to medium and, while the pan is warming, add garlic and cook for 1 minute. Using a slotted spoon, remove and discard garlic. Increase the heat to medium-high and add spinach. Cook, tossing constantly, for 1 minute. Add white wine, season with salt and pepper and cook, tossing constantly, until spinach is tender and liquid has evaporated, about 2 minutes.

To serve Cut lamb in ½-inch-thick slices and arrange on a serving platter. Top with the roasted shallots and surround it with the sautéed spinach. Serve immediately.

Irish **Stew**

with Guinness-Marinated Lamb Sirloin
and Gorgonzola Cheese

1 lb lamb sirloin, in 1-inch cubes

1 can (14.9 oz/440 mL) Guinness beer

2 bouquets garnis (each with 2 sprigs
thyme, 1 bay leaf and 1 Tbsp whole black
peppercorns wrapped in cheesecloth)

1 Tbsp extra-virgin olive oil

1 Tbsp butter

5 oz pancetta,
roughly chopped (about 1 cup)

1 large white onion,
in ½-inch dice (1½ to 2 cups)

1 medium carrot,
in ½-inch dice (about ½ cup)

2 cups beef stock

4 small Yukon Gold potatoes,
in ½-inch dice (about 2 cups)

1 cup crumbled Gorgonzola cheese

TRADITIONALLY made with mutton and cooked over an open fire, this
updated version of Irish stew is comfort food at its best. Eat while enjoying
a tall glass of Guinness. Begin the day before you plan to serve this dish to
allow time for the meat to marinate. Serves 4 to 6

Arrange lamb cubes in a glass or ceramic container with a lid and cover with
the Guinness. Bury 1 bouquet garni in with the meat and marinate lamb,
covered, in the refrigerator for 24 hours.

Preheat the oven to 325°F. Drain the lamb over a medium bowl, reserving
the beer marinade. Discard the bouquet garni. With a paper towel, pat the lamb
dry and season with salt and black pepper.

Heat a large Dutch oven or a heavy-bottomed braising pan on medium-high
and add olive oil and butter. Add lamb cubes (in batches, if necessary, to avoid
crowding in the pan) and sear on all sides for 2 to 3 minutes total, or until the
pieces are browned. Using a slotted spoon, transfer lamb to a bowl and set aside.

Add pancetta to the pan. Cook for 2 to 3 minutes, stirring, then add onions
and continue to cook for another 5 minutes until onions begin to soften.
Add carrots, the second bouquet garni, beef stock and the reserved Guinness
marinade. Without increasing the heat, bring the liquid to a boil, then cover the
pot and transfer to the oven for 2 hours. Add potatoes and cook for another
30 minutes. Remove from the heat.

Discard the bouquet garni. Strain the liquid into a small pot and reduce
by half on medium heat, to about 1¼ cups. Season with salt and pepper.

Heat the pot of meat and vegetables on medium-high, add the reduced sauce
and heat through. Divide the stew into bowls, top with crumbled Gorgonzola
cheese and serve. Without the cheese topping, the stew will keep refrigerated
in an airtight container for up to 3 days.

Pork Piccata

with White Wine–Braised Kale

Pork piccata

1 lb pork tenderloin

1 lemon

½ cup all-purpose flour

½ tsp salt

¼ tsp black pepper

3 Tbsp extra-virgin olive oil

½ cup dry white wine

¼ cup fresh lemon juice

3 Tbsp unsalted butter

2 Tbsp capers, rinsed

¼ cup finely chopped fresh flat-leaf parsley

White wine–braised kale

1 lb kale

3 Tbsp extra-virgin olive oil

2 slices pancetta or other smoked bacon, in ¼-inch dice

2 shallots, finely minced

4 cloves garlic, finely minced

½ cup dry white wine

½ cup chicken stock (page 155)

¼ cup apple cider vinegar

½ tsp salt

¼ tsp black pepper

¼ tsp dry chili flakes (optional)

THIS is one my favourite recipes in the book. My wife is a huge fan of piccata—small thin slices of meat sautéed in butter and finished with lemon juice and parsley—and because pork is such great value, we made this dish (without the wine) for the kids one day. It turned out perfectly. This is not a hard recipe to make: the key here is to use lots of lemon and lots of garlic with the kale.

If you don't have any kale, substitute rapini instead. **Serves 4**

Pork piccata Cut tenderloin crosswise into 2-oz medallions (about 8 pieces, depending on size of tenderloin).

Cut 2 pieces of plastic wrap, each 12 × 16 inches. Place 1 sheet of plastic wrap on a clean work surface. Arrange medallions, cut side down, on top and cover with the second piece of plastic wrap. Using a meat mallet, pound pork medallions to about ¼-inch thickness.

Cut both ends off the lemon, then peel away the rind and white pith and discard them. Using a small sharp knife and holding the lemon over a bowl, gently cut between the membranes and drop the segments into the bowl as they are released. Discard the membranes. Set lemon segments aside.

Place flour in a small shallow bowl. Season medallions with salt and black pepper, then dredge in flour, shaking off any excess. *Continued overleaf >*

Heat a large, heavy frying pan on medium and add olive oil. When the oil is shimmering, place pork medallions into the pan. Sauté 2 to 3 minutes on each side, browning them well. Using a slotted spoon, transfer the seared pork to a medium bowl.

Drain off any excess fat from the frying pan and add white wine and lemon juice. With a wooden spoon, scrape up any bits from the bottom of the pan. Bring the liquid to a boil, reduce the heat to medium-low, add butter and swirl to create a sauce. Add capers, parsley and lemon segments. Season to taste and keep warm on low heat.

Braised kale Wash kale well. Remove the thick ribs and chop kale roughly.

Heat a large frying pan or pot on medium heat and add 2 Tbsp of the olive oil. Place pancetta (or other bacon) in the pot and cook until crispy, about 3 minutes. Add shallots and garlic and cook for 1 minute. Add kale and stir constantly until it starts to shrink in volume, about 2 minutes. Add white wine, chicken stock and apple cider vinegar, then season with the salt, black pepper and chili flakes. Cook for 12 to 15 minutes, uncovered (so kale retains its green colour), until softened but slightly crunchy.

To serve Drain any remaining liquid from kale and place kale in the centre of a serving platter. Drizzle with the remaining olive oil. Arrange pork medallions around kale and drizzle with the sauce. Leftovers will keep refrigerated in an airtight container for up to 2 days.

Brined, Grilled **Pork Chops**

with Apple-Pineapple Relish and
Braised Brussels Sprouts

Pork Chops

¼ cup kosher salt

½ cup sugar

4 cups water

1 Tbsp crushed black peppercorns

1 bunch fresh thyme

2 bay leaves

4 double-cut pork chops, each 12 to 14 oz

2 tsp extra-virgin olive oil

Apple-Pineapple Relish

½ cup diced Granny Smith apple

1 Tbsp fresh lemon juice

½ cup diced pineapple

1 Tbsp rice vinegar

1 Tbsp liquid honey

⅓ cup roasted pecans, lightly crushed

Braised Brussels Sprouts

1 cup diced good-quality
maple-smoked bacon

2 Tbsp finely chopped shallots

1 lb Brussels sprouts,
cleaned and thinly sliced

1 Tbsp butter

Juice of ½ lemon (about 1 Tbsp)

2 Tbsp freshly grated Parmesan cheese

PORK has been part of my family's repertoire for as long as I can remember: Mom made her famous pork roast every Sunday. My wife and I love pork as well, but we brine it first for at least twenty-four hours to keep the meat very moist and hard to overcook. The relish mixes apples with sweet pineapple, then gets a nice kick of heat from chili flakes and a bit of acid from rice vinegar. Combined with Brussels sprouts—cooked at the last minute with bacon, a touch of lemon and a hint of Parmesan cheese to finish—this is a flavourful, well-rounded dish. Serve these chops with some roasted potatoes or even polenta (page 61) as well. Serves 4

Pork chops To brine pork, combine salt, sugar and the 4 cups water in a large glass or enamel bowl, mixing until dissolved. Add peppercorns, thyme and bay leaves and refrigerate until cold, about 30 minutes. Place pork chops in a large resealable bag, cover with brine and close tightly. Place the bag in a large bowl and refrigerate for 24 hours.

Apple-pineapple relish In a large bowl, toss apple with lemon juice until well coated. Add pineapple, rice vinegar and honey and set aside. This relish will keep (without the pecans, which are added just before serving) refrigerated in an airtight container for up to 4 days. *Continued overleaf >*

Finish pork chops Preheat a barbecue grill to 400°F. Line a plate with paper towels. Using tongs, remove pork chops from the brine and set on the lined plate to absorb any liquid. (If the pork chops are damp, the meat will flame on the barbecue.) Discard the brine. Allow pork chops to come to room temperature, 15 to 20 minutes, then season with salt and black pepper and brush lightly with olive oil.

Grill chops for 5 minutes, then turn them 45° and cook for another 5 minutes. Turn chops over, and grill for 5 minutes, then turn them 45° and grill for 5 minutes more. Insert a meat thermometer; once the meat reads 160°F, immediately remove chops from the heat and allow to rest for 5 minutes.

Braised Brussels sprouts Line a small plate with a paper towel. In a medium frying pan on medium heat, cook bacon until lightly crispy, about 5 minutes. (If the meat begins to smoke, reduce the heat.) Remove bacon from the pan and drain on the lined plate. Carefully pour off some of the rendered fat, then add shallots and cook for another 2 minutes. Stir in Brussels sprouts and cook for 2 more minutes, then add bacon and butter and toss lightly. Season with salt, black pepper and lemon juice. Remove from heat and stir in Parmesan cheese

To serve Fold pecans into the apple-pineapple relish. Divide the Brussels sprouts mixture among each of 4 plates. Place a pork chop over the sprouts and spoon a tablespoon of the apple mixture on top. Serve immediately.

Dry-Rubbed
Pork Shoulder Roast

1 Tbsp ground cumin

1 Tbsp garlic powder

1 Tbsp onion powder

1 Tbsp chili powder

1 Tbsp cayenne pepper

1 Tbsp freshly ground black pepper

1 Tbsp sweet paprika

½ cup brown sugar, packed

½ cup coarse salt

1 pork shoulder, bone in, 7 to 10 lbs

Pork shoulder is also known as pork butt. Buy it bone-in for more flavour and because it is actually very easy to remove the bones. Roasting the meat in the oven overnight works well for this recipe. Covering the pork allows it to release its own juices, creating steam inside the roasting pan, which helps cook the meat evenly. Serve the roast with vegetables or grains, or pull it into individual pieces to make pork sliders (page 39), garnish salads or add to tacos or sandwiches. Serves 12 to 15

In a small bowl, combine cumin, garlic powder, onion powder, chili powder, cayenne, black pepper, paprika, brown sugar and salt and mix well.

Preheat the oven to 250°F. Using your hands, rub pork shoulder generously with the rub, then place in a roasting pan. Cover tightly with aluminum foil or a lid and cook for 8 to 10 hours, until meat is fork tender and falling from the bone. Remove from the oven.

To pull, or break the meat into individual pieces, allow pork to cool slightly. When it is cool enough to handle, use your hands or a fork to pull it into long lean "threads." Wrap the pork in plastic wrap in portion-size amounts and then place in resealable plastic bags. Refrigerate for up to 3 days or freeze for up to 1 month.

Marinated **Veal Chops**

with Roasted Garlic and
Herbed Nugget Potatoes

Marinated veal chops

3 Tbsp extra-virgin olive oil

4 veal chops, each 6 to 8 oz

Zest of 2 lemons

4 to 6 garlic cloves, finely chopped

1 bunch fresh thyme

2 Tbsp unsalted butter

1 Tbsp fresh lemon juice

VEAL chops have always been one of my favourite meats, ever since we put half a calf on a spit when I was a kid visiting my uncle on his farm in Saskatchewan. The delicate meat is tender and so juicy. Here I marinate the chops and serve them with some wonderful roasted garlic and simple herbed potatoes. This is good eats!

Start this dish the morning of the day you plan to serve it, so the veal has at least six hours to marinate. Serve it family-style on a large warm serving platter. **Serves 4**

Marinated veal chops Cut a 12- × 24-inch piece of plastic wrap. Using a pastry brush, apply 1 Tbsp of the olive oil to all surfaces of the veal chops. Season them generously with salt and freshly ground black pepper.

In a small bowl, combine lemon zest and garlic, then rub evenly on each chop.

Lay out plastic wrap on a clean work surface. Cover with one-fifth of the sprigs of thyme (distributed evenly about the length and width of a veal chop) then top with one veal chop. Scatter the same amount of thyme on top of the meat. Place another veal chop on top of the first and repeat the layering of thyme and meat, ending with a layer of thyme. Tightly fold plastic wrap over the stacked chops, tucking in the ends like an envelope, and fold over once to completely encase the meat. (Use more plastic wrap if necessary.) Refrigerate for at least 6 hours to allow flavours to meld.

Roasted garlic Preheat the oven to 325°F. Leaving the garlic heads whole, chop through the top quarter of the cloves, exposing some of the flesh, and brush the cut surfaces with olive oil. Season the heads evenly with salt, black pepper, lemon juice and thyme. Place heads in a small casserole dish, cover with aluminum foil and bake for about 1 hour, until garlic is tender. Remove from the oven and set aside, leaving the foil on to keep warm, until ready to use.

Roasted garlic

4 whole heads garlic

2 tsp extra-virgin olive oil

¼ tsp salt

⅛ tsp freshly ground black pepper

1 Tbsp fresh lemon juice

2 tsp chopped fresh thyme

Herbed nugget potatoes

1 lb baby nugget potatoes, cut in half

¼ tsp salt

⅛ tsp freshly ground black pepper

2 Tbsp mascarpone cheese

1 Tbsp capers, rinsed and roughly chopped

1 Tbsp chopped fresh flat-leaf parsley

1 Tbsp extra-virgin olive oil

1 Tbsp balsamic vinegar

Finish veal Remove veal chops from the refrigerator, unwrap meat and remove but reserve thyme sprigs. Allow meat to rest at room temperature for about 15 minutes before cooking.

Place a heavy-bottomed frying pan on high heat and add the remaining 2 Tbsp of olive oil. When the oil is hot, add veal chops and sear on both sides until golden brown, about 3 minutes per side. Reduce the heat to medium-low, add butter, lemon juice and 2 to 3 pieces of reserved thyme, then baste chops constantly for about 2 minutes. Cook for about 5 minutes longer, or until veal has an internal temperature of 130 to 135°F when checked with a meat thermometer. Allow to rest in a warm place for about 10 minutes. (Veal is at its best when not overcooked; after resting, it will be medium to medium-rare.)

Herbed nugget potatoes Keep a large bowl warm. Bring a large pot of salted water to a boil on high heat. Rinse potatoes under cold running water and place them in the boiling water. Reduce the heat to medium and cook for about 10 minutes, or until tender but still holding their shape. Drain potatoes in a colander and transfer to the warm bowl. Season potatoes with the salt and pepper and stir in mascarpone cheese. Squeeze garlic from 3 of the roasted heads into the potatoes, and add capers and parsley. Mix until well combined.

To serve Place veal chops in the middle of a warm serving platter. Arrange nugget potatoes around the meat and garnish with cloves from the remaining head of roasted garlic. Drizzle with oil and balsamic vinegar. Serve immediately.

Braised **Osso Buco**

with Olive and Caper Jus

6 veal shanks, each 2 inches thick

6 Tbsp extra-virgin olive oil

1 onion, in ¼-inch dice (about 1 cup)

2 carrots, peeled,
in ¼-inch dice (about 1 cup)

2 ribs celery, in ¼-inch dice (about ¾ cup)

2 cups dry red wine

4 cups veal stock (page 156)

2 cloves garlic, minced

6 canned Roma tomatoes, crushed

Zest of 1 lemon

2 bay leaves

1 sprig fresh rosemary

5 sprigs fresh thyme

1 Tbsp capers, rinsed

½ cup green olives,
rinsed, pitted and chopped

⅛ cup chopped fresh parsley

⅛ cup chopped fresh chives

Osso buco literally means "bone with a hole" and it is prized for the succulent flavour that comes from the marrow. I have always loved this dish, and Mario Batali makes one of the best. This version is similar to his and will certainly satisfy fans of this meat.

Traditionally, osso buco is made with veal shanks cut from the top of the thigh, which has a higher proportion of meat to bone. The shank is then cross-cut into sections about two inches thick. Make sure the butcher gives you good-quality hind shanks, which are meatier than the fore ones, then cook the meat slowly and for a long time. The caper and olive jus goes just beautifully with this meat. Serve it with risotto or soft polenta (page 61). Serves 6

Preheat the oven to 325°F.

Cut 6 pieces of kitchen string, each 20 to 22 inches long. Lay out one piece of string, vertically, on a clean work surface. Place a shank on top, cross the string over the meat and tie it like a package to keep the meat in shape and on the bone. Repeat with the remaining shanks. Using paper towels, pat each shank dry then season with salt and black pepper. In a large frying pan, heat olive oil on medium heat, add shanks (in batches, if necessary, to prevent crowding the pan) and sear both sides until well browned, 3 to 4 minutes per side. Transfer shanks to a large roasting pan or a Dutch oven.

Add onions, carrots and celery to the frying pan and cook until they are golden brown and soft, about 10 minutes. Add red wine and cook for 3 more minutes. Pour the vegetable-wine mixture over the veal shanks. Add veal stock, garlic, tomatoes, lemon zest, bay leaves, rosemary and thyme to the pan, then cover tightly with a lid or aluminum foil. Place the roasting pan (or Dutch oven) in the oven and cook for 3 to 3½ hours, or until veal shanks are fork tender.

Transfer cooked shanks to a large bowl and set aside. Strain the braising liquid through a fine-mesh sieve into a large saucepan. Discard the solids. Skim the fat off the top of the braising liquid and then cook on medium-high heat until reduced by half, about 15 minutes. (You should have about 2 cups. Add a little water, if you have much less.) Stir in capers and olives. Reduce the heat to low, then return shanks to the sauce to heat through. Just before serving, add parsley and chives.

Transfer shanks to a clean work surface, cut off and discard the kitchen string and arrange on a serving platter. Pour the sauce over the shanks and serve.

Will keep refrigerated in an airtight container for up to 2 days.

Rabbit *in Tarragon Mustard Sauce*

½ lb chanterelle mushrooms

1 rabbit, about 3 lbs, in 10 pieces
(2 front leg pieces, 4 hind leg pieces
and 4 saddle pieces with ribs attached)

¼ cup all-purpose flour

4 Tbsp unsalted butter

¼ cup brandy

½ medium onion,
in ¼-inch dice (about ½ cup)

1 cup chicken stock (page 155)

3 green onions, in ¼-inch slices

¼ cup minced fresh tarragon leaves

3 Tbsp Dijon mustard

3 Tbsp mustard seeds

Juice of 1 lemon (about 2 Tbsp)

1 cup whipping cream

¼ cup minced fresh flat-leaf parsley

My first try at both cooking and eating rabbit was when I was just eighteen, and I loved its simple, lean, beautiful chicken-like flavour. One of the classic ways to prepare rabbit is with mustard, and here I share with you a version that is over-the-top good served with plain pappardelle noodles tossed in a little butter. If chanterelle mushrooms are out of season, use criminis, hedgehogs or any combination of wild and cultivated fresh mushrooms.

Most butchers these days carry rabbit. It will be whole and skinned, with the head off. Ask the butcher to cut it into the ten pieces for you, if you prefer. Serves 4

Wipe mushrooms with a damp cloth to rid them of dirt. Remove and discard any woody stems and slice mushrooms ¼ inch thick. Set aside.

Wash rabbit pieces under cold water and pat dry with paper towels. (Since rabbits have many small bones, feel the cut edges with your fingers and discard any tiny loose pieces of bone.)

Place flour on a large flat plate. Season rabbit pieces with salt and pepper, then dredge them in flour, shaking off any excess. Set rabbit aside on a clean plate.

Preheat the oven to 375°F.

Melt 3 Tbsp of the butter in a large cast-iron frying pan on medium-high heat. Add rabbit pieces and brown on all sides, 3 to 4 minutes per side. Remove the frying pan from the heat and carefully add brandy. Keeping your head away from the pan and using a barbecue lighter or a long match, ignite brandy and gently shake the pan until the flame dies. Transfer the rabbit pieces to a shallow baking dish.

Melt the remaining 1 Tbsp butter in the frying pan on medium heat. Add diced onions and cook, stirring, for 2 to 3 minutes or until translucent. Add mushrooms and cook 5 minutes, stirring often. Pour in chicken stock and deglaze the pan, then pour the mixture over the rabbit pieces. Sprinkle with green onions and tarragon. Cover and bake for 45 to 55 minutes, or until rabbit is tender and juices run clear when rabbit is cut with a knife. (The internal temperature of the thigh meat should be 165°F.)

Arrange rabbit pieces on a serving platter and cover loosely with aluminum foil to keep them warm. Combine leftover roasting juices and mushrooms in a small pot. Stir in mustard, mustard seeds, lemon juice and whipping cream. Bring the mixture to a boil on medium-high heat and reduce the sauce until it coats the back of a spoon, 5 to 6 minutes. Pour the sauce over the rabbit and sprinkle with parsley. Serve immediately. Leftovers will keep refrigerated in an airtight container for up to 2 days.

DESSERTS

Chocolate **Brownies**

with Bourbon-Butterscotch Sauce

Chocolate brownies

8 oz unsweetened chocolate,
roughly chopped

1 cup unsalted butter,
room temperature

1 vanilla bean

5 large eggs

3 cups granulated sugar

2 Tbsp vanilla extract

1 cup all-purpose flour

½ tsp salt

1 cup walnuts, roughly chopped

Bourbon-butterscotch sauce

½ cup + 2 Tbsp unsalted butter

1¼ cups whipping cream

1 vanilla bean, split in
half and seeds scraped

2 cups golden brown sugar, packed

½ cup bourbon

1 Tbsp fresh lemon juice

MY KIDS can never get enough of these rich fudge brownies, so when we make them they last maybe an hour. If you can resist eating them all at once, keep a batch in the freezer so you've always got a delicious dessert on hand. You can make these brownies into a very decadent dessert by warming up some of the bourbon-butterscotch sauce, drizzling it over the brownies and serving the whole thing with a scoop of vanilla ice cream on top. **Makes 12 brownies**

Chocolate brownies Preheat the oven to 350°F. Grease a 9- × 13-inch baking pan and line it with parchment paper, allowing the ends to extend up above the sides of the pan. (This will make it easier to remove the brownies from the pan.)

In a double boiler over hot (not boiling) water, melt chocolate and butter. Remove from the heat and set aside.

Using a small knife, slit vanilla bean lengthwise and scrape seeds into a small bowl. Discard vanilla pod (or use it to scent a container of granulated sugar).

Combine eggs, sugar, vanilla extract and vanilla seeds in a large bowl and stir until well blended. Using a spatula, fold in flour and salt, then add the melted chocolate mixture. Fold in walnuts, then pour into the greased pan, smoothing the top. Bake for 40 minutes, or until a toothpick or paring knife inserted into the centre comes out clean. The top should be firm when touched lightly. Set on a wire rack and allow to cool in the pan.

Cut into twelve 3- × 4-inch pieces, trimming the edges. Wrap leftovers in plastic wrap or waxed paper and keep at room temperature for up to 3 days or freeze for up to 1 month.

Bourbon-butterscotch sauce In a large heavy pot, combine butter, whipping cream, vanilla seeds and brown sugar. Bring to a simmer on medium-low heat, stirring often. When butter has melted, allow the mixture to bubble for 2 minutes. (The cream rises very quickly as it heats, so keep an eye on this sauce as it cooks so it does not boil over.) Remove the pot from the heat and carefully add bourbon. Keeping your head away from the pot and using a barbecue lighter or a long match, ignite bourbon and gently shake the pot until the flame dies.

Continue cooking until sauce starts to thicken, about 5 minutes (it will thicken a bit more as it cools). Finish with lemon juice.

To serve Warm each brownie in the microwave on medium-high heat for 20 seconds. Spoon 1 Tbsp warm butterscotch sauce on each plate, place a brownie on top and drizzle with another 1 Tbsp sauce. Serve with a scoop of vanilla ice cream.

Strawberry **Shortcake**

3 pints fresh strawberries
(6 cups washed, patted dry and
destemmed, the rest washed
and saved for garnish)

½ cup + 2 Tbsp granulated sugar

2¼ cups all-purpose flour

4 tsp baking powder

¼ tsp salt

⅓ cup butter

1 large egg, beaten

⅔ cup whole milk

2 cups whipped heavy cream

Around Father's Day in June, when strawberries are in full swing in B.C., one of my mother's favourite things to make is strawberry shortcake. My sister assembles the shortcake, Mom mixes the strawberries with whipped cream and when you put it all together you get one of the best desserts around. It's so simple, but at the same time so darn good.

My very first job, at fourteen, was in the food court at the Pacific National Exhibition here in Vancouver. I was working at a place called Fisher Scones that served fresh-baked scones with butter and jam all day long. Every night we were allowed to bring the leftovers home (my mom and dad loved me for that, as for two weeks they had fresh scones every morning for breakfast). What I most remember, though, is that on one side of the stand we would take the warm scones, crumble them and mix them with, yes, strawberries and whipped cream. Man, they were good.

This recipe is my version of strawberry shortcake, based on those two memories. It's a little bit of a twist on the traditional dish and a little more work than a regular shortcake recipe, but it is a real treat. Enjoy. Serves 6 to 8

Preheat the oven to 425°F. Grease and flour an 8-inch round cake pan. Slice the 6 cups strawberries and toss with the ½ cup sugar. Set aside at room temperature.

In a medium bowl, combine flour, baking powder, salt and the 2 Tbsp sugar. Using a pastry blender, cut butter into the mixture until it resembles coarse crumbs. Make a well in the centre, add egg and milk and stir until just combined. Gently gather together the dough with your hands, pat it evenly into the cake pan and bake for 15 to 20 minutes or until golden brown. Remove from the oven, set on a wire rack and allow to cool for 10 minutes in the pan. Remove cake from the pan and transfer to a large serving plate.

Using a very sharp knife, slice horizontally through the cake, making two layers. Arrange half the sliced strawberries on the bottom layer of cake, cover with the second layer and top with the remaining strawberries. Cover cake with whipped cream, then cut into wedges to serve. Garnish with the reserved berries.

Rob's Chocolate **Pots de Crème**

6 oz bittersweet chocolate, finely
chopped (70% cocoa works well)

⅔ cup granulated sugar

1 cup whole milk

1½ cups whipping cream

6 large egg yolks

2 Tbsp icing sugar, for dusting

FORGET what you think you know about chocolate pudding. If you love chocolate, make this French dessert, which kicks it up to a whole new level. Make sure you start making this dish the day before you want to serve it, as the pot de crème mixture should rest overnight. Serves 10

Place chocolate in a medium heatproof bowl. In a medium pot, combine sugar and milk on medium heat. Just before milk boils (when steam rises from the centre of the pot and bubbles form all around the edge) remove from the heat and pour over chocolate. Allow to stand for 5 minutes, then stir the melted chocolate into the milk mixture. Allow to cool for another 5 to 10 minutes, then stir in whipping cream. Allow to cool to room temperature.

Place egg yolks in a large bowl. Pour the cooled chocolate mixture into the egg yolks and mix until well combined. Cover with plastic wrap and refrigerate overnight. (Resting the pot de crème mixture overnight makes it creamier.)

Preheat the oven to 275°F. Boil a large kettle of water. Have ready ten ½-cup ramekins.

Using a spoon, skim and discard any foam that has formed on top of the mixture. Stir gently to combine. Divide the mixture among the ramekins, then place the ramekins in a baking pan. (You may need two 9-inch-square pans to hold all the ramekins.) Fill the baking pan(s) with enough hot water to come two-thirds up the sides of the ramekins. Bake for 30 to 40 minutes, or until centres move slightly when the ramekins are gently jiggled. Remove from the oven and allow to stand for 5 minutes, then transfer the ramekins to a rack and allow to cool. Refrigerate, covered with plastic wrap, for about 1 hour. Just before serving, use a fine-mesh sieve to lightly dust the top of each pot de crème with icing sugar. The pots de crème will keep refrigerated for 1 to 2 days.

Cheddar Cheese **Apple Pie**

1 recipe pâte brisée (page 163), chilled for at least 2 hours

3 lbs Gala apples (7 to 8)

½ cup granulated sugar + 1 Tbsp for garnish

¼ cup brown sugar, packed

2 Tbsp all-purpose flour

1 cup sharp extra-old Cheddar cheese, grated

WHO said too many cooks spoil the pie? This recipe is a result of the combined efforts of my mom, Cactus Club Cafe pastry chef Wendy Boys and myself, and what we have come up with is an apple pie that's to die for. The Cheddar cheese is a tribute to my mother, Margaret, who makes the best pies on the planet. Serves 8

CHEF'S TIP Oven temperatures vary widely, and pastry can quickly become tough if it is overcooked. Check on the progress of your baking often, especially the first time you make a recipe, and reduce the oven temperature if necessary.

Have ready a 9-inch pie plate. Line a baking sheet with parchment paper.

On a clean, lightly floured work surface, use a rolling pin to roll out two-thirds of the dough into a 13-inch round, about ⅛ inch thick. Place the dough into the 9-inch pie plate and trim the edges. Roll out the remaining dough into an 11-inch round, about ⅛ inch thick, and place on the baking sheet. Cover the 2 pastry rounds with plastic wrap and refrigerate until firm, about 30 minutes. While the pastry is chilling, make the filling.

Preheat the oven to 425°F. Peel and core apples, then slice them into thin wedges about ¼ inch thick. In a medium bowl, toss apples with sugars and flour.

Once the pastry has chilled, arrange apples in the pie plate, heaping the fruit higher in the middle to create a nice dome shape. Lightly brush the edges of the pie shell with water. Place the 11-inch round of pastry over the fruit and, using a sharp knife, trim off any excess dough (discard it, or roll out this leftover dough, cut it into shapes, sprinkle with sugar and bake until golden). Press the 2 layers of pastry together and, using a fork or your fingers, crimp the edges to seal the filling. Lightly brush the top of the pie with water and sprinkle with the 1 Tbsp of sugar. Cut decorative vents in the top crust to allow steam to escape. Place the pie on the lined baking sheet to catch any drips, then bake for 20 minutes. Reduce the oven temperature to 375°F and bake for another 50 to 60 minutes, or until filling is bubbling and crust is a deep golden brown. Allow the pie to cool to room temperature.

Just before serving, preheat the oven to 300°F. Cut pie into individual servings and place on ovenproof plates. Sprinkle each serving with 2 Tbsp cheese and heat in the oven until pie is slightly warm and cheese has melted.

Orange **Crème Brûlée**

8 large egg yolks

⅔ cup + 2 Tbsp granulated sugar

4 cups whipping cream

¼ cup orange brandy or orange liqueur such as Grand Marnier, Cointreau, Triple Sec or Curaçao

Zest of 2 oranges

CRÈME brûlée, or burnt sugar, is a rich custard with a caramelized sugar topping. It should be made a day or two ahead to allow for chilling between steps. Use a kitchen blowtorch, if you have one, instead of the oven broiler. Fresh fruit pairs very well with this decadent dessert. Serves 10

In a large heatproof bowl, whisk egg yolks and the ⅔ cup of sugar until well combined.

In a medium heavy pot, heat whipping cream on medium heat. Just before it boils (when steam rises from the centre of the pot and bubbles form all around the edge), remove from the heat.

Whisking constantly, slowly pour one-third of the cream in a fine stream into the egg mixture to temper it. Continue whisking, slowly adding the remaining cream, and mix well. Add brandy (or liqueur) and orange zest and allow to cool. Cover the mixture with plastic wrap, refrigerate and allow to infuse at least 12 hours or overnight.

Preheat the oven to 250°F. Boil a large kettle of water. Have ready ten ½-cup ramekins. Strain the infused cream through a fine-mesh sieve into a clean bowl, then divide the mixture among the ramekins. Place the ramekins in a large baking pan (you may need two 9-inch square pans to hold all the ramekins) and fill the baking pan(s) with enough hot water to come two-thirds up the sides of the ramekins. Bake for 45 minutes, or until centres move slightly when the ramekins are gently jiggled. Remove ramekins from the baking pan and allow to cool on a rack. Refrigerate, covered with plastic wrap, for 3 hours or overnight.

Preheat the oven broiler, setting the rack high so the top of the ramekins will be close to the heat. Place the ramekins on a baking sheet. Dividing the 2 Tbsp of sugar evenly among the brûlées, sprinkle it lightly on top, then broil until the sugar is caramelized, about 30 seconds. Watch carefully so the brûlées do not burn. Allow the brûlées to rest for a few minutes or refrigerate them for up to 4 hours before serving. Refrigerate leftover brûlées in an airtight container for up to a day.

Baklava with Walnuts
and Brandy-Soaked Prunes

2 cups granulated sugar

3 cups water

1 cup liquid honey

1 lemon, in ⅛-inch slices

1 cup brandy

1 lb dried pitted prunes

2 cups finely chopped walnuts

1 lb frozen phyllo pastry, thawed

½ cup unsalted butter, melted

THIS recipe takes me back to my days in Greece. I was eighteen and more than anything I wanted to find a bakery that sold baklava. The very first one I located was amazing: it was right in the heart of Athens and the baklava was *full* of walnuts. The prunes are my addition. (This prune-walnut mixture is also delicious as a topping on ice cream or with yogurt, or even with cheese.)

Start this dessert the morning of the day you plan to serve it, or make it up to one week ahead, wrapping it tightly in plastic wrap and keeping it in the refrigerator so it's ready to serve. Making baklava is not difficult, but it does take time. Remember to thaw frozen phyllo pastry overnight in the refrigerator or for five hours at room temperature. Serves 12 (48 pieces)

Make a simple syrup by combining sugar and 2 cups of the water in a small pot. Heat on low and stir until sugar dissolves, about 5 minutes, then increase the heat to medium and bring to a boil. Reduce the heat to low and simmer, without stirring, for 5 minutes. Stir in honey, and simmer for just 1 minute. Remove from the heat, add lemon slices and allow to cool. Transfer to an airtight container and refrigerate for 1 to 2 hours, or until chilled.

In a medium bowl, combine brandy with the remaining 1 cup of water. Add prunes and allow to soak at room temperature for 1 hour. Drain prunes, discarding the soaking liquid, then chop finely. (They should be about the same size as the chopped walnuts.) In a small bowl, combine prunes and walnuts. Set aside.

Preheat the oven to 350°F. Have a damp towel to cover the unused phyllo sheets, a pastry brush and all your ingredients ready to go. You'll want to work quickly so the phyllo pastry does not dry out.

On a large 12- × 18-inch baking pan, place one sheet of phyllo pastry and brush with melted butter. Set a second sheet of phyllo on the first and brush it with butter. Repeat with 2 more sheets of pastry, brushing each one with melted butter. Spread half the prune-walnut mixture evenly across the pastry. Layer another 2 buttered sheets of phyllo on top. Spread the remaining prune-walnut mixture over the pastry. Cover the filling with 4 sheets of buttered phyllo.

Using a small sharp knife and starting at one corner of the pan, cut pastry on a diagonal in lines about 1½ inches apart, making sure to cut through all layers, and then repeat from the opposite direction to form diamond-shaped pieces. Bake for about 30 minutes, or until golden brown. Remove from the oven.

While the baklava is still hot, remove and discard lemon slices from the syrup. Drizzle cold syrup all over the pastry and allow to cool to room temperature before serving.

Baked **Rhubarb**

1 lb rhubarb, cleaned,
with tops and ends removed

½ cup granulated sugar

1 vanilla bean, scraped
and seeds reserved

THIS simple recipe makes a light, tart dessert that is delicious served with cheesecake, plain yogurt or ice cream. If you prefer a sweeter version, use up to one cup of sugar per pound of rhubarb. Serves 6

Using a very sharp knife, slice rhubarb into ½-inch angled slices. Place rhubarb in a medium bowl.

In a small bowl, toss sugar with vanilla seeds, using your fingers to break up the seeds and distribute them evenly throughout the sugar. Add this vanilla sugar to the sliced rhubarb, cover loosely with plastic wrap or a clean kitchen towel and allow to macerate at room temperature for about 30 minutes, or until juices are released from the rhubarb.

Preheat the oven to 350°F. Uncover rhubarb, transfer to an ovenproof baking dish, stir and then bake for 30 to 40 minutes until fruit is tender and the juices are bubbling and syrupy. Serve warm, chilled or at room temperature. Will keep refrigerated in an airtight container for up to 5 days.

Crustless **Cheesecake**

3 pkgs (each 8 oz)
cream cheese, room temperature

1 cup granulated sugar

1 Tbsp cornstarch

4 large eggs

1 large egg yolk

1 cup sour cream

1 Tbsp vanilla extract

A GOOD cheesecake is a little slice of creamy indulgence. For best results with this recipe, use blocks of Philadelphia cream cheese (rather than spreadable varieties) warmed to room temperature. Do not use a convection oven to bake this dessert (it dries out).

Purists can serve this cheesecake as is, or with a fresh fruit coulis, but I recommend two variations: one flavoured with Nutella, the other with pumpkin purée. Use a table knife to fold a third of a cup of Nutella into the batter along with the vanilla extract, swirling it lightly to create a marbled effect. Alternatively, replace the sour cream in the original recipe with one cup pumpkin purée, then spice the batter with a half teaspoon each of ginger and cinnamon and a quarter of a teaspoon of nutmeg. Serves 10 to 12 (one 9-inch cake)

Set the oven rack in the middle position, then preheat the oven to 300°F. Lightly grease the bottom of a 9-inch springform pan. Cut an 18-inch square sheet of aluminum foil, then place it on a clean work surface. Set the springform pan in the middle of the foil, then snugly fold the foil up around the sides of the pan. Place the pan into a large roasting pan. Boil a large kettle of water.

In the bowl of a stand mixer fitted with a paddle attachment, combine cream cheese, sugar and cornstarch on low speed, scraping the sides of the bowl often, until the mixture is smooth. Add eggs one at a time, mixing only until combined. Fold in egg yolk, then stir in sour cream and vanilla. Scrape the mixture into the springform pan. Fill the roasting pan with enough hot water to reach halfway up the springform pan, then bake cheesecake for 90 minutes, or until the top springs back lightly to the touch. The centre may wiggle a bit when moved.

Carefully remove the springform pan from the roasting pan and transfer it to a wire rack to cool. Run the tip of a sharp knife between the cake and the pan to loosen the top edge of the cake. This prevents the cake from sticking to the pan and cracking as it cools.

When the cake is cool, about 45 minutes, carefully remove the sides of the springform pan. Place the cake, still on its springform bottom, on a large serving platter. Cut into wedges and serve immediately, or refrigerate it until chilled. Will keep refrigerated in an airtight container for up to 4 days.

Summer Berry *Marmalade*

2 cups fresh raspberries

2 cups fresh blackberries

2 cups fresh blueberries

½ cup granulated sugar

1 vanilla bean, both pod and seeds

Juice of 1 lemon (about 2 Tbsp)

1 sprig fresh mint, in chiffonade

THIS marmalade tastes like summer! Make a simple shortcake by serving it with sponge cake and whipped cream, or drizzle it over ice cream, or serve as an accompaniment to a cheese platter. Refrigerate any leftover marmalade in an airtight container for two to three days. Serves 8 or more

Place 1 cup each of raspberries, blackberries and blueberries in a small bowl. Toss gently to combine and set aside.

Using a sharp knife, cut all remaining berries in half. Set aside.

In a medium saucepan, combine the whole berries with sugar, vanilla pod and seeds and lemon juice. Bring to a boil on medium heat, stirring every 2 minutes. After 6 to 8 minutes, when the mixture is boiling to the point it cannot be stirred down, remove from the heat. Allow to cool for 5 minutes.

Remove and discard the vanilla pod. Use a spatula to gently stir in the halved berries, then allow to cool completely at room temperature.

Just before serving, fold mint into the marmalade, then serve in individual bowls.

BASICS

Fish **Stock**

Fish stock, or fumet as it's called in French, is quick and easy to make, and is a really great base for fish soups and chowders as well as seafood risottos and sauces.

The best fish bones for stock are those from mild, lean, white fish, such as halibut or cod. Fish to avoid are salmon, trout, mackerel or other oily, fatty fish because they make stock with a greasy taste.

As with any stock, be sure the bones are well rinsed with cold water. When the water runs clear, you will know that no blood remains on the bones. Pat the bones dry with a paper towel and, using a very sharp, very heavy knife, cut them into three- or four-inch pieces. Makes 8 to 9 cups

2 Tbsp grapeseed oil

2 ribs celery, in ½-inch dice (about ¾ cup)

1 onion, in ½-inch dice (about 1 cup)

1 bulb fennel, in ½-inch dice (about 1 cup)

2 to 3 leeks, white and light green parts, in ½-inch dice (about 2 cups)

4 lbs fish bones, well rinsed

1 cup dry white wine

8 cups cold water

1 bouquet garni (3 whole black peppercorns, 4 parsley stems, 1 bay leaf and 1 sprig thyme wrapped in cheesecloth)

In a heavy-bottomed stockpot, heat grapeseed oil on medium heat. Reduce the heat to low, add celery, onions, fennel and leeks and cook without browning for 5 to 10 minutes, or until onions are soft and slightly translucent. Add fish bones, cover the pot and cook for 2 to 3 more minutes, until the bones are slightly opaque. Pour in white wine and bring to a simmer. Add water and bouquet garni and simmer for 30 to 40 minutes. Using a spoon, skim any impurities from the surface.

Fill a large roasting pan with ice water and set aside. Line a fine-mesh sieve with cheesecloth and set it over a large clean bowl.

Using tongs, remove and discard fish bones. Remove stock from the heat and strain it through the sieve into the bowl. Discard the vegetables and any other solids. Set the bowl of stock in the ice water to cool quickly, for safety reasons. When stock is completely cool, pour into airtight containers and refrigerate for 2 to 3 days or freeze for up to 2 months. (Thaw frozen stock in the refrigerator before using it.)

Chicken **Stock**

Chicken stock is one of the most versatile products in any kitchen, as it's used as a base for soups and sauces, as a cooking liquid for risottos and rice pilafs, and as a braising liquid for poultry and vegetables.

This recipe is for light chicken stock, which is useful in soups and sauces. To make a dark chicken stock, which is sometimes used in sauces for poultry or veal (often as a replacement for veal stock), follow the recipe for veal stock on page 156, using chicken bones in place of veal.

When making chicken stock, keep in mind these simple tips:
- Necks, backs and wings make excellent chicken stock.
- Starting with cold water helps extract more collagen, giving the stock more body, depth of flavour and texture.
- Stock should be gently simmered not boiled so the fat rises to the top rather than emulsifying back into the liquid.
- Stock should not be stirred as it simmers because it will become cloudy and less digestible. Instead, just skim any impurities off the top with a slotted spoon, and if the liquid level drops add enough cold water to cover the bones.
- Straining the stock through a cheesecloth-lined sieve removes sediment and makes it very clear and light.
Makes 12 to 14 cups

3 lbs chicken bones

1 onion, in ¼-inch dice (about 1 cup)

2 carrots, in ¼-inch dice (about 1 cup)

2 ribs celery, in ¼-inch dice (about ¾ cup)

1 bouquet garni (1 sprig thyme, 3 to 4 parsley stems, 3 to 4 whole black peppercorns and 1 bay leaf wrapped in cheesecloth)

Rinse chicken bones well in cold water, then transfer to a heavy-bottomed stockpot. Add enough cold water (14 to 16 cups) to the pot to completely cover the bones, then bring to a boil on medium-high heat. Reduce the heat to a gentle simmer on low and, using a slotted spoon, skim off and discard any impurities that rise to the surface.

Add onions, carrots, celery and bouquet garni and continue to simmer for 3 hours, occasionally skimming impurities from the surface. Be sure bones are covered with water at all times (add more cold water, if necessary).

Fill a large roasting pan with ice water and set aside. Line a fine-mesh sieve with cheesecloth and set it over a large clean bowl.

Remove stock from the heat and strain it through the sieve into the bowl. Discard the bones, vegetables and any other solids. Set the bowl of stock in the ice water to cool quickly, for safety reasons. When stock is completely cool, skim any last fat from the surface, pour into airtight containers and refrigerate for up to 4 days or freeze for up to 3 months. (Thaw frozen stock in the refrigerator before using it.)

Veal **Stock**

Good veal stock should be gelatinous when cooled and dark and rich in colour. To make dark chicken stock, use this method, substituting chicken bones for veal. The flavour differs from veal stock but it may be used in recipes calling for veal stock, if necessary. Makes 10 to 12 cups

1 Tbsp vegetable oil

4 lbs veal bones, cracked or cut by butcher

2 onions, each cut into 8 sections

2 carrots, in 1-inch dice (about 1 cup)

2 ribs celery, in 1-inch dice (about ¾ cup)

1 large leek, washed, in 1-inch slices

6 cloves garlic, peeled

20 cups cold water

1 bouquet garni (3 sprigs thyme, 2 sprigs rosemary, 3 parsley stems, 10 whole black peppercorns and 1 bay leaf wrapped in cheesecloth)

Preheat the oven to 450°F. Set the oven rack at its lowest position.

Place vegetable oil in a large roasting pan, add veal bones and toss them lightly until well coated. Roast, stirring often to ensure even cooking, until golden brown, about 30 minutes. Add onions, carrots, celery, leeks and garlic and roast until vegetables are golden brown and bones are well browned, about 15 minutes more.

Transfer the bones and vegetables to a large stockpot and cover with 19 cups of the cold water. Add bouquet garni. Pour the remaining cup of water into the roasting pan. Using a wooden spoon, scrape the bottom of the pan to free the caramelized bits stuck there. Pour the water and browned bits into the stockpot. Bring to a boil on high, then as soon as the stock begins to boil, reduce the heat to a gentle simmer on low. Use a slotted spoon to skim off and discard any impurities that rise to the surface. Simmer for 4 hours, skimming occasionally. Be sure bones are covered with water at all times (add more cold water, if necessary).

Fill a large roasting pan with ice water and set aside. Line a fine-mesh sieve with cheesecloth and set it over a large clean bowl.

Remove stock from the heat and strain it through the sieve into the bowl. Discard the bones, vegetables and any other solids. Set the bowl of stock in the ice water to cool quickly, for safety reasons. When stock is completely cool, skim any last fat from the surface, pour into airtight containers and refrigerate for up to 4 days or freeze for up to 2 months. (Thaw frozen stock in the refrigerator before using it.)

Compound **Butter**

Compound butter is simply butter with an added flavour or two mixed in, but it is not just like buttering an item and then adding a sprinkle of the flavour. Compound butter actually becomes a unique flavour unto itself. One of the simplest examples is honey butter, a simple blend of honey with butter, whipped together and served immediately. Serving these butters is an easy way to look like you went to a lot of trouble.

Some people like to spread the flavoured butter onto a sheet of plastic wrap or waxed paper, form it into a cylinder, roll it up tightly, twisting the ends tightly, and refrigerate it for 1 hour (or freeze it for 30 minutes) so it becomes a solid roll to slice and serve with bread. With any of these variations, though, you can just whip together the ingredients in a bowl and serve. Quick to prepare, compound butters can be spread on bread for sandwiches or served with grilled meat or fish. They give toast a new spin and are delicious melted into pan juices to make rich and creamy sauces. Wrapped compound butter will keep refrigerated for up to 2 days or frozen for up to 1 month. (If frozen, cut several slices and allow them to soften at room temperature, rewrapping and returning the unused portion to the freezer.)

Each recipe makes a bit more than ½ cup

Chive butter

Serve this butter with steamed vegetables or spread on sandwiches, cooked meats, poultry or fish.

½ cup unsalted butter, softened

2 tsp capers, rinsed

1 small bunch chopped fresh chives

1 tsp sweet paprika

Juice of ½ lemon (about 1 Tbsp)

In a small bowl, use a fork to mix butter, capers, chives, paprika and lemon juice until thoroughly combined. Season to taste with salt and pepper.

Garlic butter

Use this version with canapés, or to make garlic bread or stuff snails, or to add a hit of garlic to any sauce. The garlic is blanched first to reduce its potency, which results in a more delicate flavour.

8 cloves garlic, peeled

½ cup unsalted butter, softened

1 Tbsp finely chopped fresh parsley

Bring a small pot of water to a boil on high heat. Add garlic and blanch for 8 minutes. Remove from the heat, drain and dry with paper towels.

Using a mortar and pestle or a blender, mash garlic until it forms a paste. In a small bowl, use a fork to mix garlic, butter and parsley until thoroughly combined. Season to taste with salt and pepper.

Lemon butter

This variation is delicious with fish.

Zest of ½ lemon

½ cup unsalted butter, softened

Juice of 1 lemon (about 2 Tbsp)

Bring a small pot of water to a boil on high heat. Add lemon zest and blanch for 2 minutes. Remove from the heat, drain and dry with paper towels. Using a sharp knife, finely chop the zest.

In a small bowl, use a fork to mix lemon zest and butter. Add lemon juice and mix well until thoroughly combined. Season to taste with salt and pepper.

Basic **Mayonnaise**

Homemade mayonnaise is easy to make and tastes lighter than store-bought varieties, but handle it carefully. Since raw eggs can contain bacteria such as salmonella, wash your hands, use only eggs without cracks in their shell and refrigerate any unused mayonnaise right away. You can double this recipe if you like. Makes 1¼ cups

CHEF'S TIP Before you whisk the grapeseed oil into the mixture, set the bowl on a damp dishcloth on the counter to prevent it from moving while you have both hands busy whisking in the oil.

1 egg yolk

1 tsp Dijon mustard

½ tsp salt

¼ tsp white pepper

1 Tbsp fresh lemon juice

1 tsp white vinegar

1 cup grapeseed oil

In a small bowl, combine egg yolk, mustard, salt, white pepper, lemon juice and white vinegar until well mixed. Whisking constantly, gradually add grapeseed oil in a thin steady stream, until the mayonnaise thickens.

Transfer to an airtight container and refrigerate for no more than 2 to 3 days.

Variations

To make the variations, mix all ingredients in a small bowl until thoroughly combined. Each recipe makes ½ cup.

Barbecue mayonnaise

This variation makes a great dipping sauce for meats, chicken and fish and is tasty in sandwiches, as well.

½ cup basic mayonnaise (page 158)

2 Tbsp quick barbecue sauce (page 160)

¼ tsp smoked paprika

½ tsp Tabasco sauce (preferably green)

Hoisin mayonnaise

Use this Asian variation with the Asian sloppy joes (page 40) and barbecued duck spring rolls (page 21).

½ cup basic mayonnaise (page 158)

2 Tbsp hoisin sauce

½ tsp sesame oil

Curry mayonnaise

This mayonnaise is a great addition to vegetarian sandwiches or it can be used as a dip for roasted vegetables or vegetable patties.

½ cup basic mayonnaise (page 158)

2 finely chopped oven-dried tomatoes (page 7)

1½ tsp finely chopped fresh cilantro

1½ tsp curry powder

2 Tbsp freshly squeezed lime juice

Sambal mayonnaise

I love spicy foods, and this mayonnaise adds punch to roasted potatoes as well as fish and chicken sandwiches.

½ cup basic mayonnaise (page 158)

2 tsp sambal oelek

Balsamic **Reduction**

This versatile sauce is delicious on salads and on grilled meats and fish. It also works well with desserts, drizzled over grilled peaches and figs or fresh berries. Makes 1 cup

3 cups balsamic vinegar

½ tsp honey

In a small heavy-bottomed pot, combine balsamic vinegar and honey and bring to a boil on medium-low heat. Reduce the heat to low and simmer until reduced to 1 cup, about 10 minutes. Will keep refrigerated in an airtight container for up to 2 months.

Ponzu **Sauce**

This sauce is widely used with seafood and makes a great dipping sauce for dumplings or spring rolls. Makes 2 cups

½ cup soy sauce

½ cup fresh lemon juice

1 cup rice vinegar

In a medium bowl, combine soy sauce, lemon juice and rice vinegar until well mixed. Transfer to an airtight container and refrigerate for up to 1 week.

Spicy Ponzu Sauce

I discovered this Japanese sauce at a very young age, and it is still one of my favourite flavours. Serve it with spring rolls or raw fish. Makes 2½ cups

2 cups ponzu sauce (page 159)

1 Tbsp + 1½ tsp Tabasco sauce
(or any vinegary spicy sauce)

¼ cup lime juice

1 Tbsp + 1½ tsp finely minced ginger

1½ tsp minced Thai chilies

1 Tbsp + 1½ tsp finely minced red onions

1 Tbsp chopped cilantro

In a medium bowl, combine all ingredients and mix well. Transfer to an airtight container and refrigerate for up to 3 days.

Quick **Barbecue Sauce**

I make double batches of this barbecue sauce because it's fun to do and suits any barbecued meat or poultry—and because my kids love it. The keys to this basting sauce are the saltiness of the soy and the sweetness of the ketchup. Makes 3 cups

⅓ cup tomato paste

¼ cup brown sugar, packed

⅓ cup molasses

⅓ cup white vinegar

⅓ cup soy sauce

⅓ cup honey

⅓ cup ketchup

1 Tbsp + 1½ tsp Dijon mustard

1 Tbsp + 1½ tsp Worcestershire sauce

1 Tbsp + 1½ tsp garlic powder

1 Tbsp + 1½ tsp onion powder

2½ cups cold water

1 to 1½ tsp hot sauce, or to taste

Combine all ingredients in a medium pot. Stir to mix well and bring to a boil on medium heat. Reduce the heat to medium-low and simmer for 10 to 15 minutes, until liquid has reduced to two-thirds and is slightly thickened. Refrigerate in an airtight container for up to 2 weeks.

Spicy **Barbecue Sauce**

The spiciness of this barbecue sauce can be altered by adjusting the amount of sambal to suit your taste. Sambal is an Indonesian and Malaysian word that means "condiment" and "side dish," and most are hot and spicy. Serve this dipping sauce with meatballs (page 118) and pulled pork sandwiches (page 39). Makes 2½ cups

2 Tbsp vegetable oil

¼ cup finely chopped onions

¼ cup finely chopped celery

½ cup finely chopped green bell peppers

2 cloves garlic, finely chopped

¼ cup brown sugar, packed

1 bay leaf

1 Tbsp Dijon mustard

¼ cup sambal oelek or to taste

2¾ cups ketchup

¾ cup canned crushed tomatoes

¼ tsp chili powder

1 Tbsp Worcestershire sauce

¼ cup honey

¼ cup red wine vinegar

Heat vegetable oil in a large pot on medium-high. Add onions, celery, bell peppers and garlic and sauté until tender, stirring frequently, 8 to 10 minutes. Reduce the heat to low and stir in brown sugar, stirring constantly until it has dissolved. Add bay leaf, mustard, sambal oelek, ketchup, tomatoes, chili powder, Worcestershire sauce, honey and red wine vinegar and stir well. Simmer for about 2 hours, stirring occasionally, until the mixture is thick and dark reddish brown. Remove from the heat and allow to cool.

Discard bay leaf then transfer to an airtight container and refrigerate for up to 1 week or freeze for up to 2 months.

Tomato and Basil **Sauce**

This is a sauce I make for my family at least twice a week. It's simple, takes less than ten minutes to prepare and tastes fresh and flavourful. We use it in almost every dish that calls for a tomato sauce. Keep this recipe handy no matter where you are. Makes 1½ cups

1 tin (14 oz) canned Roma tomatoes

2½ Tbsp extra-virgin olive oil

⅓ cup basil, in chiffonade

Over a medium bowl, gently crush tomatoes with your hands to break them up and release the juices. Set aside.

Heat olive oil in a small pan on medium-high. Add basil and cook for 30 seconds. Add tomatoes and simmer gently for 5 to 10 minutes. Season to taste with salt.

Will keep refrigerated in an airtight container for up to 3 days.

Roasted Tomato **Sauce**

The tomatoes in this recipe are roasted for several hours to intensify their flavour before making the sauce, but you can do this ahead of time and refrigerate them, covered, until you need them (or for up to three days). Use the ripest tomatoes you can find. Makes 4 cups

20 Roma tomatoes

1½ tsp salt

1 Tbsp chopped fresh thyme

¼ cup extra-virgin olive oil

2 cups onions, in ¼-inch dice

2 Tbsp minced garlic

1 cup tomato juice

1 Tbsp finely chopped fresh sage

⅔ tsp black pepper

¼ cup roughly chopped fresh basil

Preheat the oven to 200°F.

Cut each tomato in half lengthwise and place it, cut side up, on a baking sheet. Sprinkle tomatoes lightly with 1 tsp of the salt and about half of the thyme. Roast in the oven for about 6 hours, then allow to cool. Peel and discard skins from tomatoes. Set aside.

Heat a large heavy-bottomed pot on medium-high and add olive oil. Add onions and sauté until translucent, 4 to 5 minutes. Stir in garlic and cook for another 2 minutes, then add roasted tomatoes and tomato juice. Add sage and bring to a boil, then reduce the heat to low and simmer for 45 minutes, stirring occasionally. Season to taste with pepper and the remaining salt, and allow to cool. Add basil and the remaining thyme to the cooled sauce to maintain its freshness.

Refrigerate in an airtight container for up to 5 days or freeze for up to 2 months.

Bolognese **Sauce**

This recipe makes one darn good sauce. It was an instant hit when I first cooked it for my staff at Lumière years ago and I still make it all the time at home.

I have to thank my good friend Pino Posteraro for showing me the real secrets of making great pasta (page 164) over which to serve this sauce. Alternatively, use it over store-bought pasta (rigatoni is ideal) to feed a crowd, as a filling for sloppy joes (page 40) or as extra protein on nachos or tacos (adding spices such as cumin and chili flakes). Serves 8 to 10 (makes 5 cups)

2 Tbsp extra-virgin olive oil

1 lb ground pork

1 lb ground veal

¼ cup diced onions

¼ cup diced carrots

¼ cup diced celery

1 tsp chopped fresh rosemary

1 tsp fresh thyme

1 tsp chopped fresh sage leaves

1 tsp minced garlic

⅓ cup tomato paste

⅓ cup orange juice

⅓ cup dry red wine

1 cup veal stock (page 156) and 1 cup dark chicken stock (page 156) OR 2 cups of either stock

2 oz pancetta, finely chopped

Heat a large stockpot on medium-high and add 1 Tbsp of the olive oil. When oil is nearly smoking, add pork and veal and sauté, stirring with a wooden spoon to break up the meat. Cook for 4 to 5 minutes, or until meat is crumbly and no longer pink. Season with salt and black pepper and transfer to a metal bowl. Set aside.

Add the remaining olive oil to the stockpot. Add onions and cook for 2 to 3 minutes, or until onions are translucent. Stir in carrots, celery, rosemary, thyme, sage and garlic and cook for another 2 to 3 minutes, or until vegetables soften and become aromatic. Return meat to the pot and mix with vegetables until well combined. Add tomato paste and mix well to coat meat and vegetables. Pour in orange juice, red wine and veal (and/or chicken) stock and bring to a boil. Reduce the heat to low and simmer, stirring occasionally, to reduce the sauce by half, about 1 hour.

While the sauce is cooking, line a plate with a paper towel. Cook pancetta in a small frying pan on medium heat until crispy. Just before serving, fold pancetta into the sauce and season to taste with salt and black pepper. Will keep refrigerated in an airtight container for up to 4 days or frozen for up to 2 months.

Pâte Brisée *(Pie Pastry Dough)*

I have been lucky to work with some great chefs, and their influence always makes me better as an all-round chef. Wendy Boys, one of Canada's best pastry chefs, helped me perfect this classic pie pastry. Keep this recipe handy, as you will share it over and over again. For best results, have everything cold and spotlessly clean, work quickly and don't overmix. Use butter rather than traditional lard (or vegetable shortening) for best flavour. **Makes 1 double- or 2 single-crust 9- to 10-inch pies**

2½ cups all-purpose flour

1 tsp salt

1 tsp granulated sugar

1 cup unsalted butter, chilled, in 1-inch cubes

¼ to ½ cup ice water

In the bowl of a food processor, combine flour, salt and sugar. Pulse briefly to mix dry ingredients. Add butter, and pulse until the mixture resembles coarse meal, 8 to 10 seconds.

With the machine running, slowly add ¼ cup ice water in a steady stream. Pulse until dough holds together without being wet and sticky (about 30 seconds). To test, stop the motor and squeeze a small amount of dough together between your fingers. If it is crumbly, add 1 Tbsp ice water and pulse in and test again. If necessary, keep adding water, 1 Tbsp at a time, until the dough just holds together when pressed between your fingers.

Lightly dust a clean work surface with flour. Cut two 15-inch lengths of plastic wrap.

Turn dough onto the work surface and gather it together with your hands. Divide into 2 equal balls. Flatten into discs and wrap each one well in plastic wrap. Refrigerate for at least 1 hour before rolling, or freeze one or both plastic-wrapped discs for up to 1 month. (Place the plastic-wrapped dough into a resealable plastic bag before putting it in the freezer.)

To roll the pastry, remove it from the refrigerator ½ hour before use. Lightly flour a work surface.

Unwrap the dough and place it on the work surface. Using a rolling pin and working from the centre to the edges, roll the pastry 3 or 4 times in one direction, lift gently with your hands and rotate a quarter turn. Repeat, dusting with additional flour as necessary, until you have an even ⅛-inch-thick disc. Roll it loosely onto the rolling pin, drape it over the pie plate and unroll. Gently fit pastry into the pie plate, pressing it firmly onto the bottom and sides. Using kitchen scissors or a sharp knife, trim overhanging dough, leaving ½ inch around all the edges.

For a single-crust pie, fold the ½-inch edge of dough under itself to make a thicker edge. Using a fork or your fingers, crimp or flute the edge. Prick the dough all over with a fork.

Pasta **Dough**

One of the secrets to my signature butternut squash ravioli is the dough that I use. Easy to make at home, this recipe will not disappoint you. Pasta dough can be mixed by hand or in a food processor (or in a stand mixer), but for best results, use a pasta machine to roll it out.
Makes ¾ lb

1½ cups all-purpose flour
+ 2 Tbsp for sprinkling and dusting

1 tsp salt

6 large egg yolks + 2 whole large eggs

1 Tbsp vegetable oil

1 tsp cold whole milk

To mix by hand, measure the 1½ cups flour onto a large, clean work surface, add salt and mix with your hands to combine. Form flour into a mound and make a well in the centre. In a medium bowl, combine egg yolks and eggs, vegetable oil and milk until eggs are just broken up. Pour this wet mixture into the well in the flour. Using a fork (or one of your hands), gradually incorporate flour into the egg mixture. To do this, push a bit of the flour on the inside of the well into the liquid and mix gently until smooth. Work your way around the inside of the well, repeating this process until all the flour has been incorporated and the dough just holds together when pressed with your fingers. (If it is too dry to stick together, add 1 tsp water at a time, mixing well, until it does.) Gather the dough into a ball. Lightly sprinkle the work surface with flour and knead the dough gently for 10 minutes until smooth.

Form into a disc 1½ inches thick, wrap in plastic wrap and allow to rest at room temperature for at least 30 minutes or for up to 1 hour, so the gluten relaxes and makes it easier to roll and softer to eat.

To mix in a food processor, fit your food processor with the steel blade. In the bowl of the food processor, place the 1½ cups flour and salt and pulse 2 or 3 times to blend. In a medium bowl, combine egg yolks and eggs, vegetable oil and milk until eggs are just broken up. With the motor running, slowly add all the egg mixture in a steady stream. When the dough just starts to hold together, turn off the motor. Pulse only until dough forms a ball. Lightly sprinkle a large clean work surface with flour and knead the dough gently for 10 minutes until smooth. Form into a disc 1½ inches thick, wrap in plastic wrap and allow to rest at room temperature for at least 30 minutes or for up to 1 hour, so the gluten relaxes and makes it easier to roll and softer to eat.

To roll and shape the dough, attach the pasta machine to a secure surface and set the roller to its widest setting, usually #1. Lightly dust a baking sheet with flour.

Unwrap pasta dough, reserving the plastic wrap, and place on a large clean work surface. Using a sharp knife, cut dough into 4 equal pieces. Rewrap 3 of the pieces.

With your hands, flatten the dough into a rectangle 3 inches wide and ½ inch thick. Thin out one end edge of the dough more than the others and feed it through the pasta roller, holding the dough with one hand and turning the handle with the other. Fold the rolled dough in thirds and flatten again. Repeat running the dough through the #1 setting and folding it several more times, lightly dusting it with flour between rollings, until the dough looks smooth. Set the roller to the next widest setting and feed the dough through (it is not necessary to fold the dough between rollings once it is smooth), repeating with thinner settings and more rollings until the pasta dough is the desired thickness. Cut into desired shapes and place on the baking sheet to dry a little before cooking.

Gnocchi

Another thing I love to make with my kids is gnocchi, the beautifully light pasta made with potatoes. The key here is to buy a ricer, which takes the lumps out of the potato and creates a soft, succulent texture. Serve gnocchi simply with a basic tomato sauce (page 161) and freshly grated Parmesan cheese. Other possibilities include a dab of butter or compound butter (pages 156–57) and a sprinkling of cheese, a dollop of summer-fresh herb pesto, or any meat or vegetable sauce or gravy. Serves 6 to 8

2 lbs Yukon Gold potatoes, unpeeled but scrubbed

2 cups all-purpose flour

1¼ cups freshly grated Parmesan cheese

1 tsp salt

¼ tsp black pepper

1 large egg

Line a baking sheet with parchment paper.

Place whole potatoes in a large pot with enough water to cover. Bring to a boil on high heat, reduce to a simmer and cook until potatoes are soft, 12 to 15 minutes. Drain and then peel potatoes while still warm, discarding the skins. For a light, fluffy texture, pass potatoes through a potato ricer or press through a sieve. (Do not use a food processor or the potatoes will become gluey.)

Place potato on a clean, lightly floured work surface and make a well in the centre. Sprinkle with flour and Parmesan cheese. Add salt and pepper. Place egg in the middle of the well and slowly, using a fork, mix egg into the potato-flour mixture. When ingredients are all incorporated, gather into a ball and knead the dough for about 5 minutes, until it feels dry to the touch.

Divide the dough into 8 to 10 small balls. Roll each ball into a rope ¾ inch in diameter. Cut into 1-inch-long pieces. Arrange cut pieces in a single layer on the baking sheet, cover with plastic wrap and freeze until solid. Transfer to an airtight container and store in the freezer for up to 2 months. (Gnocchi do not need to be thawed before cooking.)

To cook gnocchi, bring a large pot of salted water to a boil on high heat. Drop gnocchi into the water in batches and cook until they float to the top of the pot, 3 to 4 minutes. Using a slotted spoon, transfer cooked gnocchi to a large bowl and add 1 tsp olive oil so they don't stick. Serve immediately or allow to cool and then refrigerate. Cooked gnocchi will keep refrigerated in an airtight container for 1 to 2 days.

METRIC CONVERSIONS

(rounded off to the nearest even whole number)

Weight

IMPERIAL OR U.S.	METRIC
1 oz	30 g
2 oz	60 g
3 oz	85 g
4 oz	115 g
5 oz	140 g
6 oz	170 g
7 oz	200 g
8 oz (½ lb)	225 g
9 oz	255 g
10 oz	285 g
11 oz	310 g
12 oz	340 g
13 oz	370 g
14 oz	400 g
15 oz	425 g
16 oz (1 lb)	455 g
2 lbs	910 g

Volume

IMPERIAL OR U.S.	METRIC
⅛ tsp	0.5 mL
¼ tsp	1 mL
½ tsp	2.5 mL
¾ tsp	4 mL
1 tsp	5 mL
1 Tbsp	15 mL
1½ Tbsp	23 mL
⅛ cup	30 mL
¼ cup	60 mL
⅓ cup	80 mL
½ cup	120 mL
⅔ cup	160 mL
¾ cup	180 mL
1 cup	240 mL

Linear

IMPERIAL OR U.S.	METRIC
⅛ inch	3 mm
¼ inch	6 mm
½ inch	12 mm
¾ inch	2 cm
1 inch	2.5 cm
1¼ inches	3 cm
1½ inches	3.5 cm
1¾ inches	4.5 cm
2 inches	5 cm
3 inches	7.5 cm
4 inches	10 cm
5 inches	12.5 cm
6 inches	15 cm
7 inches	18 cm
12 inches	30 cm
24 inches	60 cm

Baking utensils

IMPERIAL OR U.S.	METRIC
5 × 9-inch loaf pan	2 L loaf pan
9 × 13-inch cake pan	4 L cake pan
11 × 17-inch baking sheet	30 × 45-cm baking sheet

Oven Temperature

IMPERIAL OR U.S.	METRIC
150°F	65°C
250°F	120°C
275°F	135°C
300°F	150°C
325°F	160°C
350°F	180°C
375°F	190°C
400°F	200°C
425°F	220°C
450°F	230°C

Liquid Measures
(for alcohol)

IMPERIAL OR U.S.	METRIC
1 oz	30 mL
1½ oz	45 mL
2 oz	60 mL
3 oz	90 mL
4 oz	120 mL